Teacher's Guide 6

William Collins' dream of knowledge for all began with the publication of his first book in 1819. A self-educated mill worker, he not only enriched millions of lives, but also founded a flourishing publishing house. Today, staying true to this spirit, Collins books are packed with inspiration, innovation and practical expertise. They place you at the centre of a world of possibility and give you exactly what you need to explore it.

Collins. Freedom to teach.

An imprint of HarperCollinsPublishers
The News Building
1 London Bridge Street
London SE1 9GF

Browse the complete Collins catalogue at
www.collins.co.uk

© HarperCollins*Publishers* Limited 2016

10 9 8 7

ISBN 978-0-00-814777-8

Jennifer Martin asserts her moral rights to be identified as the author of this work.

All rights reserved. No part of this publication may be reproduced, stored in a retrieval system, or transmitted in any form by any means, electronic, mechanical, photocopying, recording or otherwise, without the prior written permission of the Publisher or a licence permitting restricted copying in the United Kingdom issues by the Copyright Licensing Agency Ltd., 90 Tottenham Court Road, London W1T 4LP.

British Library Cataloguing in Publication Data
A catalogue record for this publication is available from the British Library.

Publisher Celia Wigley
Publishing manager Karen Jamieson
Commissioning editor Lucy Cooper
Series editor Karen Morrison
Managing editor Caroline Green
Editor Amanda Redstone
Project managed by Emily Hooton
Edited by Karen Williams
Proofread by Cassie Fox
Cover design by Amparo Barrera
Cover artwork by Tomislav Zlatic
Internal design by Ken Vail Graphic Design
Typesetting by Ken Vail Graphic Design and Contentra Technologies India Private Limited
Illustrations by Ken Vail Graphic Design, Advocate Art and Beehive Illustration
Production by Robin Forrester and Lyndsey Rogers

Printed and bound by CPI Group (UK) Ltd, Croydon, CR0 4YY

Contents

Section 1 Introduction

About Collins International Primary English	5
Assessment in primary English	6
Formal written assessment	7
Learning objectives matching grid	8

Section 2 Unit-by-Unit Support

Unit 1: Backwards and forwards

Unit overview	21
Learning objectives	21
Related resources	22
Week 1	23
Week 2	26
Week 3	28

Unit 2: Family matters

Unit overview	30
Learning objectives	30
Related resources	31
Week 1	31
Week 2	34
Week 3	36

Unit 3: From pencils to pixels

Unit overview	39
Learning objectives	39
Related resources	40
Week 1	40
Week 2	43
Week 3	47

Unit 4: It's about time

Unit overview	52
Learning objectives	52
Related resources	53
Week 1	54
Week 2	58
Week 3	60

Unit 5: Facts, foibles and fables
Unit overview	62
Learning objectives	62
Related resources	63
Weeks 1 and 2	64
Weeks 1 and 2 (continued)	68
Week 3	69

Unit 6: Holey-moley
Unit overview	72
Learning objectives	72
Related resources	74
Week 1	74
Week 2	76
Week 3	78

Unit 7: Stop!
Unit overview	82
Learning objectives	82
Related resources	83
Week 1	83
Week 2	86
Week 3	88

Unit 8: I spy
Unit overview	90
Learning objectives	90
Related resources	91
Week 1	91
Week 2	95
Week 3	97

Unit 9: Sporting chance
Unit overview	99
Learning objectives	99
Related resources	100
Week 1	100
Week 2	102
Week 3	104

Section 3 Photocopiable masters (PCMs)

PCM 1–26	**108**
Formal assessment 1	**139**
Formal assessment 2	**143**
Formal assessment 3	**149**

Introduction

About Collins International Primary English

Collins International Primary English is specifically written to fully meet the requirements of the Cambridge Primary English curriculum framework, and the material has been carefully developed to meet the needs of primary English learners and teachers in a range of international contexts.

The material at each level has been organized into nine units, each based around particular text types. The activities in each unit are introduced and explored in contexts related to the selected texts.

The course materials are supplemented and enhanced by a range of print and electronic resources, including photocopiable (printable) master sheets for support, extension and assessment of classroom based activities (you can find these on pages 108 to 138 of this Teacher's Guide as well as on the digital resource) and a range of interactive digital activities to add interest and excitement to learning. Reading texts are supported by audio files.

Components of the course

For each of Stages 1–6 as detailed in the Cambridge Primary English curriculum framework, we offer:

- a full colour, highly illustrated Student's Book with integral reading texts
- a write-in Workbook linked to the Student's Book
- this comprehensive Teacher's Guide with clear instructions for using the materials and interactive digital package, which includes warm-up presentations, audiofiles of readings, interactive activities and record keeping for teacher use only.

Approach

The course is designed with learner-centred learning at its heart. Learners work through a range of contextualised reading, writing, speaking and listening activities with guidance and support from their teacher. Plenty of opportunity is provided for learners to consolidate and apply what they have learned and to relate what they are learning both to other contexts and the environment in which they live.

Much of learners' work is conducted in pairs or small groups in line with international best practice. The tasks and activities are designed to be engaging for learners and to support teachers in their assessment of learner progress and achievement. Each set of lessons is planned to support clear learning objectives and the activities within each unit provide opportunities for oral and written feedback by the teacher as well as self- and peer-assessment options.

Throughout the course, there is a wide variety of learning experiences on offer. The materials are organized so that they do not impose a rigid structure, but rather allow for a range of options linked to the learning objectives.

Differentiation

Differentiation in the form of support and extension ideas is built into the unit-by-unit teaching support in this Teacher's Guide.

Achievement levels are likely to vary from learner to learner, so we have included a graded set of assessment criteria in each weekly review section. The **square**, **circle** and **triangle** assessment criteria indicate what learners at varying levels might be expected to have achieved each week. **Square** indicates what can be expected of almost all learners. **Circle** indicates what might be expected of most learners, and **triangle** indicates what level of achievement might be expected from more able learners. Levels will vary as some learners may find some topics more interesting and/or easier; similarly, some may excel at speaking activities rather than written ones.

Teacher's Guide

The Teacher's Guide offers detailed guidance for covering each unit. Each unit is designed to cover three teaching weeks. The teacher knows their class and context best, so they should feel free to vary the pace and the amount of work covered each week to suit their circumstances. Each unit has a clear structure, with an introduction, suggestions for introducing the unit, learning objectives and a resource list of supporting materials that can be used in the unit.

Student's Book

The Student's Book offers a clear structure and easy-to-follow design to help learners to navigate the course. The following features are found at all levels:

- A range of fiction, non-fiction, poetry, play scripts and transactional texts are provided to use as a starting point for contextualized learning.
- Skills-based headers allow teachers to locate activities within the curriculum framework and indicate to learners what skills are being focussed on in each task.
- Clear instruction rubrics are provided for each activity. The rubrics allow learners to develop more and more independent learning as they begin to master and understand instructive text. The rubrics also model assessment type tasks and prepare them for formal assessment at all levels.
- Icons indicate where there is an audio-visual support for the text. Teachers can play these to the class and learners can use these themselves if they need to listen to the text again.
- Grammar and language boxes provide teaching text and examples to show the language feature in use. These are colour coded so that learners can easily recognize them as they work through the course.
- The notepad feature contains reminders, hints and interesting facts.
- *Thinking Deeper* boxes contain additional information and encourage learners to apply what they have been learning in different contexts or in more challenging ways. These are clearly signposted in the text.

Workbook

The workbook is clearly linked to the Student's Book. The activities here contain structured spaces for learners to record answers. The activities can be used as classroom tasks, for homework, or for assessment purposes. The completed workbook tasks give the teacher an opportunity to check work and give written feedback and/or grades. Learners have a consolidated record of their work and parents can see what kind of activities learners are doing in class.

Digital resources

The digital resources are offered online by subscription. You can access these at Collins Connect. These resources can be used to introduce topics and support learning and assessment.

The interactive activities include:

- drag and drop activities
- matching activities
- look-cover-say-spell activities
- cloze procedure (fill in the missing words)
- labelling diagrams
- and many more.

Learners receive instant feedback when they complete the activities and the responses are randomized so learners can complete the tasks they enjoy more than once, getting a different arrangement of items each time.

Some materials can be printed out for use in the classroom. These include a set of additional activity sheets that can be used for support, extension and/or homework as well as an additional assessment task for each unit. (These tasks are teacher marked.)

Collins Connect offers an easy and accessible method of keeping records. Teachers can compile class lists and keep track of progress in an easy-to-use and well-supported system.

Using the audio files in the classroom

All of the reading and listening texts in the course have been recorded and are supplied with the digital subscription as audio files. These offer a range of voices, pace and expression and they will enhance the classroom experience by introducing variety and making it easier for the teacher to observe learners as they listen to, and follow texts. The audio files can also be accessed in the student-only view so learners who are struggling with reading can listen to these on their own as many times as they like.

We suggest that you use the audio files as you introduce each reading text. Learners can either listen only or follow in their books as they listen to the text. Following and listening allows them to hear the words and the correct pronunciation and also to get a sense of where to pause, where to change expression and how to pace themselves when reading aloud.

Assessment in primary English

In the primary English programme, assessment is a continuous, planned process that involves collecting information about learner progress and learning in order to provide constructive feedback to both learners and parents and also to guide planning and the next teaching steps.

The Cambridge Primary English curriculum framework makes it clear what learners are expected to learn and achieve at each level. Our task as teachers is to assess whether or not learners have achieved the stated goals using clearly focussed, varied, reliable and flexible methods of assessment.

In the Collins International Primary English course, assessment is continuous and in-built. It applies the principles of international best practice and ensures that assessment:

- is ongoing and regular
- supports individual achievement and allows for learners to reflect on their learning and set targets for themselves
- provides feedback and encouragement to learners
- allows for integration of assessment into he activities and classroom teaching by ombining different assessment methods, including observations, questioning, self-assessment and formal and informal tasks/tests
- uses strategies that cater for a variety of learner needs in the classroom (language, physical, emotional and cultural), and acknowledges that learners do not all need to be assessed at the same time, or in the same way
- allows for, and prepares learners for, more formal summative assessment including controlled activities, tasks and tests.

Formal written assessment

The Collins International Primary English course offers a set of assessment sheets that teachers can use to formally assess learning and to award marks if necessary. These sheets test the skills and competencies developed in a cumulative manner. In some cases, learners will use the same texts as context. In other cases, they will be expected to read and make sense of an unseen text and to answer a range of contextualized questions based on that.

At Stage 6, there is an end of unit review (test) at the end of units 3, 6 and 9. These are accompanied by a mark scheme.

In addition to the materials supplied in the course, schools may opt for their learners to take standardized Cambridge Primary progression tests at Stages 3, 4, 5 and 6. These tests are developed by Cambridge Assessment International Education but they are written and marked in schools. Teachers download tests and administer them in their own classrooms. Cambridge International provides a marks scheme and you can upload learners' test results and then analyse the results and print reports. You can also compare a learner's results against their class, school or other schools around the world and on a year-by-year basis.

Learning objectives matching grid

The types of reading texts and the objectives covered in each unit are listed here by strand for easy reference. These same objectives are listed in full at the beginning of each unit in the unit-by-unit support section of this guide.

Unit 1	Reading	Writing	Listening and speaking
Backwards and forwards Texts *Hall of the Bulls*, extended narrative with time shift *The Tear Jar*, extended narrative *Volcanoes*, non-fiction, formal and impersonal *Pompeii Times*, journalistic writing	6R01 Articulate personal responses to reading, with close reference to the text. 6R02 Revise different word classes. 6R03 Develop familiarity with the work of established authors and poets, identifying features which are common to more than one text. 6Rx1 Distinguish between fact and opinion in a range of texts and other media. 6Rx2 Paraphrase explicit meanings based on information from more than one point in the text. 6Ri1 Consider how the author manipulates the reaction of the reader, e.g. how characters and settings are presented. 6Ri2 Look for implicit meanings, and make plausible inferences from more than one point in the text. 6Rw1 Comment on a writer's use of language, demonstrating awareness of its impact on the reader. 6Rw3 Analyse the success of writing in evoking particular moods, e.g. suspense. 6Rw7 Understand aspects of narrative structure, e.g. the handling of time. 6Rw8 Analyse how paragraphs and chapters are structured and linked.	6W01 Continue to learn words, apply patterns and improve accuracy in spelling. 6Wa3 Explore definitions and shades of meaning and use new words in context. 6Wa4 Use the styles and conventions of journalism to write reports on events. 6Wa7 Adapt the conventions of the text type for a particular purpose. 6Wa8 Select appropriate non-fiction style and form to suit specific purposes. 6Wa10 Summarise a passage, chapter or text in a given number of words. 6Wa12 Use different genres as models for writing. 6Wp4 Develop increasing accuracy in using punctuation effectively to mark out the meaning in complex sentences. 6Wp5 Punctuate speech and use apostrophes accurately. 6Ws1 Learn word endings with different spellings but the same pronunciation, e.g.	6SL1 Express and explain ideas clearly, making meaning explicit and respond to guidance about, and feedback on, the quality of contributions. 6SL2 Use spoken language well to persuade, instruct or make a case, e.g. in a debate. 6SL3 Vary vocabulary, expression and tone of voice to engage the listener and suit the audience, purpose and context. 6SL5 Speak confidently in formal and informal contexts. 6SL6 Pay close attention in discussion to what others say, asking and answering questions to introduce new ideas. 6SL8 Prepare, practise and improve a spoken presentation or performance.

	6Rw11 Explore use of active and passive verbs within a sentence. 6Rw13 Identify use of dashes. 6Rv1 Recognise key characteristics of a range of non-fiction text types.(News report) 6Rv3 Revise language conventions and grammatical features of different types of text. 6Rv4 Compare the language, style and impact of a range of non-fiction writing.	-tion, -cian, -sion, -ssion; **-ance**, -ence. 6Ws4 Develop knowledge of word roots, prefixes and suffixes, including recognising variations, e.g. *im*, *in*, *ir*, *il*; *ad*, *ap*, *af*, *al* and knowing when to use double consonants. 6Ws5 Know how to transform meaning with prefixes and suffixes.	
Unit 2	**Reading**	**Writing**	**Listening and speaking**
Family matters Texts *Amparo's Journey*, fiction, playscript *Spud*, fiction, diary extract Gran can you rap? poem The man in the park, poem	6R01 Articulate personal responses to reading, with close reference to the text. 6R02 Revise different word classes. 6Rx2 Paraphrase explicit meanings based on information from more than one point in the text. 6Ri1 Consider how the author manipulates the reaction of the reader, e.g. how characters and settings are presented. 6Ri2 Look for implicit meanings, and make plausible inferences from more than one point in the text. 6Rw1 Comment on a writer's use of language, demonstrating awareness of its impact on the reader. 6Rw2 Explore proverbs, sayings and figurative expressions. 6Rw3 Analyse the success of writing in evoking particular moods, e.g. suspense.	6W01 Continue to learn words, apply patterns and improve accuracy in spelling. 6Wa1 Establish and maintain a clear viewpoint, with some elaboration of personal voice. 6Wa2 Develop some imaginative detail through careful use of vocabulary and style. 6Wa3 Explore definitions and shades of meaning and use new words in context. 6Wa4 Use the styles and conventions of journalism to write reports on events. 6Wa7 Adapt the conventions of the text type for a particular purpose. 6Wa12 Use different genres as models for writing. 6Ws1 Learn word	6SL1 Express and explain ideas clearly, making meaning explicit and respond to guidance about, and feedback on, the quality of contributions. 6SL3 Vary vocabulary, expression and tone of voice to engage the listener and suit the audience, purpose and context. 6SL5 Speak confidently in formal and informal contexts. 6SL6 Pay close attention in discussion to what others say, asking and answering questions to introduce new ideas. 6SL8 Prepare, practise and improve a spoken presentation or performance. 6SL9 Convey ideas about characters in drama in different roles and scenarios through deliberate choice of speech, gesture and movement.

	6Rw4 Begin to show awareness of the impact of a writer's choices of sentence length and structure.	endings with different spellings but the same pronunciation, e.g. *-tion, -cian, -sion, -ssion; -ance, -ence*.	
	6Rw6 Discuss and express preferences in terms of language, style and themes.		
	6Rw9 Read and interpret poems in which meanings are implied or multilayered.		
	6Rw10 Explore how poets manipulate and play with words and their sounds.		
	6Rw13 Identify uses of brackets.		
Unit 3	**Reading**	**Writing**	**Listening and speaking**
From pencils to pixels Texts *David Copperfield*, fiction, extended narrative *Malala Yousafzai*, non-fiction, autobiography and blog *Perspective*, non-fiction formal and impersonal *The hole in the wall project*, non-fiction, biography and journalistic writing	6R01 Articulate personal responses to reading, with close reference to the text. 6R02 Revise different word classes. 6Rx1 Distinguish between fact and opinion in a range of texts and other media. 6Rx2 Paraphrase explicit meanings based on information from more than one point in the text. 6Ri1 Consider how the author manipulates the reaction of the reader, e.g. how characters and settings are presented. 6Ri2 Look for implicit meanings, and make plausible inferences from more than one point in the text. 6Rw1 Comment on a writer's use of language, demonstrating awareness of its impact on the reader.	6W01 Continue to learn words, apply patterns and improve accuracy in spelling. 6Wa1 Establish and maintain a clear viewpoint, with some elaboration of personal voice. 6Wa3 Explore definitions and shades of meaning and use new words in context. 6Wa6 Develop skills of writing biography and autobiography in role. 6Wa7 Adapt the conventions of the text type for a particular purpose. 6Wa12 Use different genres as models for writing. 6Wp4 Develop increasing accuracy in using punctuation effectively to mark out the meaning in complex sentences.	6SL1 Express and explain ideas clearly, making meaning explicit and respond to guidance about, and feedback on, the quality of contributions. 6SL5 Speak confidently in formal and informal contexts. 6SL6 Pay close attention in discussion to what others say, asking and answering questions to introduce new ideas. 6SL7 Help to move group discussion forward, e.g. by clarifying, summarising.

	6Rw5 Understand the use of conditionals, e.g. to express possibility. 6Rw6 Discuss and express preferences in terms of language, style and themes. 6Rw12 Understand changes over time in words and expressions and their use. 6Rv1 Recognise key characteristics of a range of non-fiction text types. 6Rv2 Understand the conventions of standard English usage in different forms of writing. 6Rv3 Revise language conventions and grammatical features of different types of text. 6Rv4 Compare the language, style and impact of a range of non-fiction writing. 6Rv5 Explore autobiography and biography, and first and third person narration. 6Rv8 Begin to develop awareness that the context for which the writer is writing and the context in which the reader is reading can impact on how the text is understood.	6Wp5 Punctuate speech and use apostrophes accurately. 6Ws1 Learn word endings with different spellings but the same pronunciation, e.g. -tion, -cian, 6Ws6 Explore word origins and derivations and the use of words from other languages.	
Unit 4	**Reading**	**Writing**	**Listening and speaking**
It's about time Texts *The Giver*, science fiction *Tuck Everlasting*, fiction, extended narrative	6R01 Articulate personal responses to reading, with close reference to the text. 6R02 Revise different word classes. 6Ri1 Consider how the author manipulates the reaction of the reader, e.g. how characters and settings are presented.	6W01 Continue to learn words, apply patterns and improve accuracy in spelling. 6Wa2 Develop some imaginative detail through careful use of vocabulary and style. 6Wa7 Adapt the conventions of the	6SL1 Express and explain ideas clearly, making meaning explicit and respond to guidance about, and feedback on, the quality of contributions. 6SL2 Use spoken language well to persuade, instruct or make a case, e.g. in a debate.

What happened to the dinosaurs? Non-fiction, formal and impersonal	6Ri2 Look for implicit meanings, and make plausible inferences from more than one point in the text. 6Rw1 Comment on a writer's use of language, demonstrating awareness of its impact on the reader. 6Rw2 Explore proverbs, sayings and figurative expressions. 6Rw3 Analyse the success of writing in evoking particular moods, e.g. suspense. 6Rw4 Begin to show awareness of the impact of a writer's choices of sentence length and structure. 6Rw5 Understand the use of conditionals, e.g. to express possibility. 6Rv3 Revise language conventions and grammatical features of different types of text. 6Rw6 Discuss and express preferences in terms of language, style and themes. 6Rw7 Understand aspects of narrative structure, e.g. the handling of time. 6Rw8 Analyse how paragraphs and chapters are structured and linked. 6Rw13 Identify uses of the semi-colon. 6Rv1 Recognise key characteristics of a range of non-fiction text types. 6Rv2 Understand the conventions of standard English usage in different forms of writing. 6Rv3 Revise language conventions and grammatical features of different types of text.	text type for a particular purpose. 6Wa12 Use different genres as models for writing. 6Wt1 Plan plot, characters and structure effectively in writing an extended story. 6Wt2 Use paragraphs, sequencing and linking them appropriately to support overall development of the text. 6Wt3 Manage the development of an idea throughout a piece of writing, e.g. link the end to the beginning. 6Wt4 Use a range of devices to support cohesion within paragraphs. 6Wp1 Use a wider range of connectives to clarify relationships between ideas, e.g. however, therefore, although. 6Wp5 Punctuate speech and use apostrophes accurately. 6Ws1 Learn word endings with different spellings but the same pronunciation, –sion, –ssion;	6SL5 Speak confidently in formal and informal contexts. 6SL6 Pay close attention in discussion to what others say, asking and answering questions to introduce new ideas.

	6Rv8 Begin to develop awareness that the context for which the writer is writing and the context in which the reader is reading can impact on how the text is understood.		
Unit 5	**Reading**	**Writing**	**Listening and speaking**
Facts, foibles and fables Texts *Phobias*, non-fiction formal and impersonal Blurb and extracts from *Weird Monsters*, non-fiction, formal and impersonal *The Fox and the Crow*, fiction, fable *Holes*, fiction, story with flashbacks *Mosquitoes*, poem	6R01 Articulate personal responses to reading, with close reference to the text. 6R02 Revise different word classes. 6R03 Develop familiarity with the work of established authors and poets, identifying features which are common to more than one text. 6Rx1 Distinguish between fact and opinion in a range of texts and other media. 6Rx2 Paraphrase explicit meanings based on information from more than one point in the text. 6Ri1 Consider how the author manipulates the reaction of the reader, e.g. how characters and settings are presented. 6Ri2 Look for implicit meanings, and make plausible inferences from more than one point in the text. 6Rw1 Comment on a writer's use of language, demonstrating awareness of its impact on the reader. 6Rw2 Explore proverbs, sayings and figurative language. 6Rw4 Begin to show awareness of the impact of a writer's choices of	6W01 Continue to learn words, apply patterns and improve accuracy in spelling. 6Wa1 Establish and maintain a clear viewpoint, with some elaboration of personal voice. 6Wa7 Adapt the conventions of the text type for a particular purpose. 6Wa8 Select appropriate non-fiction style and form to suit specific purposes. 6Wa9 Write non-chronological reports linked to work in other subjects. 6Wa12 Use different genres as models for writing. 6Wt1 Plan plot, characters and structure effectively in writing an extended story. 6Wt2 Use paragraphs, sequencing and linking them appropriately to support overall development of the text. 6Wt4 Use a range of devices to support cohesion within paragraphs.	6SL1 Express and explain ideas clearly, making meaning explicit and respond to guidance about, and feedback on, the quality of contributions. 6SL5 Speak confidently in formal and informal contexts. 6SL6 Pay close attention in discussion to what others say, asking and answering questions to introduce new ideas. 6SL7 Help to move group discussion forward, e.g. by clarifying, summarising. 6SL8 Prepare, practise and improve a spoken presentation or performance. 6SL9 Convey ideas about characters in drama in different roles and scenarios through deliberate choice of speech, gesture and movement.

		sentence length and structure. 6Rw5 Understand the use of conditionals, e.g. to express possibility. 6Rw8 Analyse how paragraphs and chapters are structured and linked. 6Rw9 Read and interpret poems in which meanings are implied or multilayered. 6Rw10 Explore how poets manipulate and play with words and their sounds. 6Rv1 Recognise key characteristics of a range of non-fiction text types. 6Rv3 Revise language conventions and grammatical features of different types of text. 6Rv4 Compare the language, style and impact of a range of non-fiction writing. 6Rv8 Begin to develop awareness that the context for which the writer is writing and the context in which the reader is reading can impact on how the text is understood.	6Wt5 Use connectives to structure an argument or discussion. 6Wp1 Use a wider range of connectives to clarify relationships between ideas, e.g. *however*, *therefore*, *although*. 6Wp2 Develop grammatical control of complex sentences, manipulating them for effect. 6Wp3 Distinguish the main clause and other clauses in a complex sentence. 6Wp4 Develop increasing accuracy in using punctuation effectively to mark out the meaning in complex sentences. 6Ws2 Use correct choices when representing consonants, e.g. 'ck'/'k'/'ke'/'que'/'ch'. 6Ws3 Further investigate spelling rules and exceptions, including representing unstressed vowels. 6Ws6 Explore word origins and derivations and the use of words from other languages. 6Ws7 Investigate meanings and spellings of connectives.	
Unit 6	**Reading**	**Writing**	**Listening and speaking**
Holey-moley	6R01 Articulate personal responses to reading, with close reference to the text.	6W01 Continue to learn words, apply	6SL1 Express and explain ideas clearly, making meaning explicit and respond to guidance

Texts			
Black holes, non-fiction, formal and impersonal

How to do a presentation, non-fiction instructions

Holes, fiction, extended narrative with flashbacks

How to do an oral report as a team, non-fiction, instructions

High flight, poem with imagery

My sister, poem | 6R02 Revise different word classes.

6R03 Develop familiarity with the work of established authors and poets, identifying features which are common to more than one text.

6Rx1 Distinguish between fact and opinion in a range of texts and other media.

6Rx2 Paraphrase explicit meanings based on information from more than one point in the text.

6Ri1 Consider how the author manipulates the reaction of the reader, e.g. how characters and settings are presented.

6Ri2 Look for implicit meanings, and make plausible inferences from more than one point in the text.

6Rw1 Comment on a writer's use of language, demonstrating awareness of its impact on the reader.

6Rw2 Explore proverbs, sayings and figurative expressions.

6Rw3 Analyse the success of writing in evoking particular moods, e.g. suspense.

6Rw4 Begin to show awareness of the impact of a writer's choices of sentence length and structure.

6Rw7 Understand aspects of narrative structure, e.g. the handling of time.

6Rw8 Analyse how paragraphs and chapters are structured and linked.

6Rw9 Read and interpret poems in which meanings are implied or multilayered. | patterns and improve accuracy in spelling.

6W02 Use handwriting and IT effectively, making appropriate choices of presentation, to prepare writing for publication.

6Wa1 Establish and maintain a clear viewpoint, with some elaboration of personal voice.

6Wa7 Adapt the conventions of the text type for a particular purpose.

6Wa12 Use different genres as models for writing.

6Wt2 Use paragraphs, sequencing and linking them appropriately to support overall development of the text.

6Wt4 Use a range of devices to support cohesion within paragraphs.

6Wt5 Use connectives to structure an argument or discussion.

6Wp1 Use a wider range of connectives to clarify relationships between ideas, e.g. *however*, *therefore*, *although*.

6Ws2 Use correct choices when representing consonants, e.g. 'ck'/'k'/'ke'/'que'/'ch'; 'ch'/'tch'; 'j'/'dj'/'dje'.

6Ws4 Develop knowledge of word roots, prefixes and suffixes, including recognising variations, e.g. im, in, ir, il; ad, ap, af, al and knowing | about, and feedback on, the quality of contributions.

6SL2 Use spoken language well to persuade, instruct or make a case, e.g. in a debate.

6SL3 Vary vocabulary, expression and tone of voice to engage the listener and suit the audience, purpose and context.

6SL4 Structure talk to aid a listener's understanding and engagement.

6SL5 Speak confidently in formal and informal contexts.

6SL6 Pay close attention in discussion to what others say, asking and answering questions to introduce new ideas.

6SL7 Help to move group discussion forward, e.g. by clarifying, summarising.

6SL8 Prepare, practise and improve a spoken presentation or performance.

6SL9 Convey ideas about characters in drama in different roles and scenarios through deliberate choice of speech, gesture and movement. |

		when to use double consonants.	
	6Rw10 Explore how poets manipulate and play with words and their sounds.		
	6Rv1 Recognise key characteristics of a range of non-fiction text types.	6Ws5 Know how to transform meaning with prefixes and suffixes.	
	6Rv2 Understand the conventions of standard English usage in different forms of writing.	6Ws7 Investigate meanings and spellings of connectives.	
	6Rv3 Revise language conventions and grammatical features of different types of text.		
	6Rv6 Identify features of balance written arguments.		
	6Rv7 Take account of viewpoint in a novel, and distinguish voice of author from that of narrator.		
	6Rv8 Begin to develop awareness that the context for which the writer is writing and the context in which the reader is reading can impact on how the text is understood.		

Unit 7	Reading	Writing	Listening and speaking
Stop! Texts *Rhino facts*, non-fiction, formal and impersonal *Rhino poaching*, non-fiction infographics, journalistic writing *Zoos*, non-fiction, argument and discussion *Arguments for and against legalising trade in rhino products*, non-fiction, argument and discussion	6R01 Articulate personal responses to reading, with close reference to the text. 6R02 Revise different word classes. 6Rx1 Distinguish between fact and opinion in a range of texts and other media. 6Rx2 Paraphrase explicit meanings based on information from more than one point in the text. 6Ri2 Look for implicit meanings, and make plausible inferences from more than one point in the text. 6Rw1 Comment on a writer's use of language, demonstrating awareness of its impact on the reader.	6W03 Develop a personal handwriting style to write legibly, fluently and with increasing speed, choosing the writing implement that is best suited for a task. 6Wa1 Establish and maintain a clear viewpoint, with some elaboration of personal voice. 6Wa5 Write a balanced report of a controversial issue. 6Wa11 Argue a case in writing, developing points logically and convincingly. 6Wa12 Use different genres as models for writing.	6SL1 Express and explain ideas clearly, making meaning explicit and respond to guidance about, and feedback on, the quality of contributions. 6SL2 Use spoken language well to persuade, instruct or make a case, e.g. in a debate. 6SL3 Vary vocabulary, expression and tone of voice to engage the listener and suit the audience, purpose and context. 6SL5 Speak confidently in formal and informal contexts. 6SL6 Pay close attention in discussion to what others say, asking and answering questions to introduce new ideas.

The Leopard Poachers, fiction, extended narrative	6Rw3 Analyse the success of writing in evoking particular moods, e.g. suspense. 6Rw4 Begin to show awareness of the impact of a writer's choices of sentence length and structure. 6Rw6 Discuss and express preferences in terms of language, style and themes. 6Rw8 Analyse how paragraphs and chapters are structured and linked. 6Rw13 Identify uses of the colon, semi-colon, parenthetic commas, dashes and brackets. 6Rv1 Recognise key characteristics of a range of non-fiction text types. 6Rv3 Revise language conventions and grammatical features of different types of text. 6Rv5 Explore autobiography and biography, and first and third person narration. 6Rv6 Identify features of balanced written arguments. 6Rv7 Take account of viewpoint in a novel, and distinguish voice of author from that of narrator.	6Wt3 Manage the development of an idea throughout a piece of writing, e.g. link the end to the beginning. 6Wt4 Use a range of devices to support cohesion within paragraphs. 6Wt5 Use connectives to structure an argument or discussion. 6Wp1 Use a wider range of connectives to clarify relationships between ideas, e.g. however, therefore, although. 6Ws2 Use correct choices when representing consonants, e.g. 'ck'/'k'/'ke'/'que'/'ch'; 'ch'/'tch'; 'j'/'dj'/'dje'. 6Ws7 Investigate meanings and spellings of connectives.	6SL7 Help to move group discussion forward, e.g. by clarifying, summarising.
Unit 8	**Reading**	**Writing**	**Listening and speaking**
I spy Texts *Virginia Hall: World War II Spy*, non-fiction, biography *Refugee Boy*, fiction, extended narrative with flashbacks	6R01 Articulate personal responses to reading, with close reference to the text. 6R02 Revise different word classes. 6R03 Develop familiarity with the work of established authors and poets, identifying features which are common to more than one text.	6W01 Continue to learn words, apply patterns and improve accuracy in spelling. 6W02 Use handwriting and IT effectively, making appropriate choices of presentation, to prepare writing for publication. 6W03 Develop a personal handwriting style to write legibly,	6SL1 Express and explain ideas clearly, making meaning explicit and respond to guidance about, and feedback on, the quality of contributions. 6SL4 Structure talk to aid a listener's understanding and engagement. 6SL5 Speak confidently in formal and informal contexts.

	6Rx2 Paraphrase explicit meanings based on information from more than one point in the text.	fluently and with increasing speed, choosing the writing implement that is best suited for a task.	6SL6 Pay close attention in discussion to what others say, asking and answering questions to introduce new ideas.
	6Ri1 Consider how the author manipulates the reaction of the reader, e.g. how characters and settings are presented.	6Wa1 Establish and maintain a clear viewpoint, with some elaboration of personal voice.	6SL7 Help to move group discussion forward, e.g. by clarifying, summarising.
	6Ri2 Look for implicit meanings, and make plausible inferences from more than one point in the text.	6Wa2 Develop some imaginative detail through careful use of vocabulary and style.	6SL8 Prepare, practise and improve a spoken presentation or performance.
	6Rw1 Comment on a writer's use of language, demonstrating awareness of its impact on the reader.	6Wa3 Explore definitions and shades of meaning and use new words in context.	6SL10 Reflect on variations in speech, and appropriate use of standard English.
	6Rw11 Explore use of active and passive verbs within a sentence.	6Wa6 Develop skills of writing biography and autobiography in role.	
	6Rv1 Recognise key characteristics of a range of non-fiction text types.	6Wa7 Adapt the conventions of the text type for a particular purpose.	
	6Rv2 Understand the conventions of standard English usage in different forms of writing.	6Wa12 Use different genres as models for writing.	
	6Rv3 Revise language conventions and grammatical features of different types of text.	6Wt2 Use paragraphs, sequencing and linking them appropriately to support overall development of the text.	
	6Rv4 Compare the language, style and impact of a range of non-fiction writing.	6Wt5 Use connectives to structure an argument or discussion.	
	6Rv5 Explore autobiography and biography, and first and third person narration.	6Wp5 Punctuate speech and use apostrophes accurately.	
	6Rv7 Take account of viewpoint in a novel, and distinguish voice of author from that of narrator.	6Ws4 Develop knowledge of word roots, prefixes and suffixes, including recognising variations, e.g. *im, in,*	
	6Rv8 Begin to develop awareness that the context for which the		

	writer is writing and the context in which the reader is reading can impact on how the text is understood.	*ir, il*; *ad, ap, af, al* and knowing when to use double consonants. 6Ws5 Know how to transform meaning with prefixes and suffixes. 6Ws6 Explore word origins and derivations and the use of words from other languages.	
Unit 9	**Reading**	**Writing**	**Listening and speaking**
Sporting chance Texts *Becoming an Olympic Gymnast*, non-fiction, autobiography *The Highwayman*, poem with imagery	6R01 Articulate personal responses to reading, with close reference to the text. 6R02 Revise different word classes. 6R03 Develop familiarity with the work of established authors and poets, identifying features which are common to more than one text. 6Ri1 Consider how the author manipulates the reaction of the reader, e.g. how characters and settings are presented. 6Ri2 Look for implicit meanings, and make plausible inferences from more than one point in the text. 6Rw2 Explore proverbs, sayings and figurative expressions. 6Rw3 Analyse the success of writing in evoking particular moods, e.g. suspense. 6Rw9 Read and interpret poems in which meanings are implied or multilayered. 6Rw10 Explore how poets manipulate and play with words and their sounds.	6W01 Continue to learn words, apply patterns and improve accuracy in spelling. 6Wa1 Establish and maintain a clear viewpoint, with some elaboration of personal voice. 6Wa2 Develop some imaginative detail through careful use of vocabulary and style. 6Wa3 Explore definitions and shades of meaning and use new words in context. 6Wa4 Use the styles and conventions of journalism to write reports on events. 6Wa5 Write a balanced report of a controversial issue. 6Wa7 Adapt the conventions of the text type for a particular purpose. 6Wa12 Use different genres as models for writing. 6Wp2 Develop grammatical control of complex sentences,	6SL1 Express and explain ideas clearly, making meaning explicit and respond to guidance about, and feedback on, the quality of contributions. 6SL2 Use spoken language well to persuade, instruct or make a case, e.g. in a debate. 6SL3 Vary vocabulary, expression and tone of voice to engage the listener and suit the audience, purpose and context. 6SL4 Structure talk to aid a listener's understanding and engagement. 6SL5 Speak confidently in formal and informal contexts. 6SL8 Prepare, practise and improve a spoken presentation or performance. 6SL9 Convey ideas about characters in drama in different roles and scenarios through deliberate choice of speech, gesture and movement. 6SL10 Reflect on variations in speech, and appropriate use of standard English.

	6Rw12 Understand changes over time in words and expressions and their use. 6Rw13 Identify uses of the colon, semi-colon, parenthetic commas, dashes and brackets. 6Rv1 Recognise key characteristics of a range of non-fiction text types. 6Rv3 Revise language conventions and grammatical features of different types of text. 6Rv5 Explore autobiography and biography, and first and third person narration.	manipulating them for effect. 6Wp4 Develop increasing accuracy in using punctuation effectively to mark out the meaning in complex sentences. 6Wp5 Punctuate speech and use apostrophes accurately. 6Ws3 Further investigate spelling rules and exceptions, including representing unstressed vowels. 6Ws4 Develop knowledge of word roots, prefixes and suffixes.	

Unit 1 Backwards and forwards

Unit overview

This is the first of nine units. Its focus is on school life, and in particular, school trips. By connecting through their own experience with the first two texts, learners will have a strong base of understanding to draw from when they interpret the texts. The two fiction texts have been structured to cross the 'conventions' of time. Whilst these are not quite science fiction stories, they do give learners the opportunity to explore the effect of time in plot development.

The third text is a non-fiction account of volcanoes: a contrast to the handling of the eruption of Pompeii in the second extract.

In addition, learners will also read some instruction texts (how to structure a debate, how to summarise a chapter and how to write a newspaper article).

You are beginning a new year, with a new class, so you may wish to use the activities in the first unit as diagnostic tasks – assessing what prior knowledge your learners have, and how well they read, understand what they are reading, and communicate with others in their groups or pairs.

Several of the language learning areas listed in the curriculum will be repeated throughout the year, but require introduction early on. These include:

- Proofreading and editing, which learners should do before they hand in each piece of writing.
- Keeping a reading log. Encourage learners to record what they have read each week – and remember to include readings from websites as well as books. Set aside a time each week for this record keeping.
- Keeping a personal dictionary. For this, each learner needs an alphabetised notebook, in which they record new words and their meanings, and difficult spelling.
- Using a dictionary or IT to check the spelling and meanings of words. Have dictionaries and/or IT available for each learner to use in the classroom.

Unit 1	Reading	Writing	Listening and speaking
Backwards and forwards Texts *Hall of the Bulls*, extended narrative with time shift *The Tear Jar*, extended narrative *Volcanoes*, non-fiction, formal and impersonal *Pompeii Times*, journalistic writing	6R01 Articulate personal responses to reading, with close reference to the text. 6R02 Revise different word classes. 6R03 Develop familiarity with the work of established authors and poets, identifying features which are common to more than one text. 6Rx1 Distinguish between fact and opinion in a range of texts and other media. 6Rx2 Paraphrase explicit meanings based on information from more than one point in the text. 6Ri1 Consider how the author manipulates the reaction of the reader,	6W01 Continue to learn words, apply patterns and improve accuracy in spelling. 6Wa3 Explore definitions and shades of meaning and use new words in context. 6Wa4 Use the styles and conventions of journalism to write reports on events. 6Wa7 Adapt the conventions of the text type for a particular purpose. 6Wa8 Select appropriate non-fiction style and form to suit specific purposes. 6Wa10 Summarise a passage, chapter or text in a given number of words. 6Wa12 Use different genres as models for writing.	6SL1 Express and explain ideas clearly, making meaning explicit and respond to guidance about, and feedback on, the quality of contributions. 6SL2 Use spoken language well to persuade, instruct or make a case, e.g. in a debate. 6SL3 Vary vocabulary, expression and tone of voice to engage the listener and suit the audience, purpose and context. 6SL5 Speak confidently in formal and informal contexts. 6SL6 Pay close attention in discussion to what others say, asking and answering

	e.g. how characters and settings are presented. 6Ri2 Look for implicit meanings, and make plausible inferences from more than one point in the text. 6Rw1 Comment on a writer's use of language, demonstrating awareness of its impact on the reader. 6Rw3 Analyse the success of writing in evoking particular moods, e.g. suspense. 6Rw7 Understand aspects of narrative structure, e.g. the handling of time. 6Rw8 Analyse how paragraphs and chapters are structured and linked. 6Rw11 Explore use of active and passive verbs within a sentence. 6Rw13 Identify use of dashes. 6Rv1 Recognise key characteristics of a range of non-fiction text types.(News report) 6Rv3 Revise language conventions and grammatical features of different types of text. 6Rv4 Compare the language, style and impact of a range of non-fiction writing.	6Wp4 Develop increasing accuracy in using punctuation effectively to mark out the meaning in complex sentences. 6Wp5 Punctuate speech and use apostrophes accurately. 6Ws1 Learn word endings with different spellings but the same pronunciation, e.g. -tion, -cian, -sion, -ssion; **-ance,** -ence. 6Ws4 Develop knowledge of word roots, prefixes and suffixes, including recognising variations, e.g. *im, in, ir, il; ad, ap, af, al* and knowing when to use double consonants. 6Ws5 Know how to transform meaning with prefixes and suffixes.	questions to introduce new ideas. 6SL8 Prepare, practise and improve a spoken presentation or performance.

Related resources

- Audio files: *Hall of the Bulls*; *Two-thousand-year-old figs*; *Volcanoes*
- PCM 1: Summary activity
- PCM 2: Debate worksheet

Week 1

Student's Book pages 1–6

Workbook pages 1–3

Introducing the unit
Project photographs of cave art onto a screen. Discuss what it must have been like to live in pre-historic times. Let learners suggest ways in which the lives of children living in pre-historic times were different from and similar to their own lives.

Student's Book page 1
Speaking and reading
1 Bring a collection of books to class and place them randomly on desks/shelves in the room. Make sure you have a wide selection, ranging from encyclopaedias to picture books. Instruct learners to look only at the covers and to write down the titles of the three books they'd most like to read. Instruct learners to sit in small groups and share their book lists with each other. Make sure that learners give reasons for their choices.

Write the title of the short story the class is about to read on the board. Discuss the class's predictions for the plot of the story they are about to read. Write some of the predictions on the board for future reference.

Workbook pages 1–2
Writing
To sharpen learners' focus and understanding of the effect of setting on a plot, let learners complete the 'setting activity'. Alternatively, this could be completed after the reading of the text.

Answers
1

The children looked through the window.	A spiteful wind was scratching at the glass, demanding to be let in. Rain crashed down, drowning their voices whilst every now and then, jagged streaks of light pierced the black sky.
	Rolling green lawns, soft as velvet, stretched out forever, dawdling aimlessly to a gentle little stream minding its own business as it trickled over smooth rocks and pebbles.
	The room did not welcome their inquisitive eyes It was dark and dull and bleak…

Student's Book pages 2–3
Speaking and reading

2 Let learners read through the text silently, making notes about the content of the chapters as they do so. Once they have read the text, discuss the accuracy, or lack thereof, of their predictions.

Student's Book page 4
Comprehension
1 Give learners time discuss the questions before writing the answers.

Answers
a About 10 as they are in Class 4C.
b Everyone had been having a lot of fun on the school trip to France. That usually meant noise – laughing, talking and shouting. Now, the students were impressed and listened carefully – they were quiet!
c The age of the paintings impressed the class. - "… over 17,000 years old"
d Open question. (to create drama/to look important)
e The paintings are brighter. The boys see a forest in place of the modern buildings.
f They tripped over a rock and hit their heads.
g Own suggestion (It's fine for learners to say they can't prove anything. You will be referring to this when you discuss debating later on in the unit.)
h Own ideas (The strange painting, Time travel, the cavemen kids)

Student's Book pages 4–5
Reading and writing
Write two headings on the board: 'FACTS' and 'OPINIONS'. To find out learners' level of understanding of these concepts, divide the class into small 'ability' groups and instruct each group to write one fact and one opinion about the story. Ask learners to explain their responses and to work out a clear definition for each concept. Based on the groups' responses, either do the following support activity or continue with the summarising activity.

Support
Facts vs opinions
Write the following sentences on the board and discuss the information they are providing.

I enjoyed the story. (opinion)

The boys were scared of the cavemen. (Incorrect fact – the boys tried to make friends by sharing food.)

The boys travelled back in time. (Fact – I don't think they have ever seen a sandwich before… I think we must have travelled back in time!)

The boys behaved badly. (opinion – the statement is open to debate)

Workbook page 3
Writing
Discuss the tips on how to write a summary. Ask learners to refer to the notes they jotted down as they read the story. In groups, let them compare the notes they made.

Give the following instructions:

- Decide what the main topic of each chapter is, and write down a sentence to describe it.
- As a group, write down the main points of chapter one.
- Decide on how to write the points in sentences.
- Check the spelling, punctuation and structure of the sentences for accuracy.
- Check that the sentences have not been copied from the text.
- Check that the paragraph is no more than 150 words.
- Repeat the process for the second chapter, but work in pairs.
- Repeat the process for the third chapter, but work individually.

PCM 1: Summary activity is available should anyone need to repeat this exercise with another text.

Extension
Reduce the number of words for in which each chapter should be summarised.

Learners could summarise information from other content subjects.

Learners create their own 'Facts vs Opinions' video.

Student's Book page 5
Spelling
Learners can play the 'Bouncing Anagram spelling game' on the Spellzone site: http://bit.ly/1F4omiK (Spellzone is an online English spelling course with many free activities for your learners.)

Answers
1 elegance; distance; abundance; arrogance; importance; tolerance; ignorance
2 When the verb ends in -*ear*, add -*ance*; if the verb begins with *a*, add -*ance*; if the verb ends in -*y*, change the -*y* to -*i* and add -*ance*.

Student's Book page 6
Reading and speaking
Refer back to the comprehension question that asked how the boys would feel if the teacher did not believe their account of their time travel adventure. Use this question to lead a short discussion about 'the right to have a voice'. Inform learners that they will be participating in classroom debates on various topics. (There are various debating formats – some allow for the audience to actively participate in the debate as well. Should you wish this, open the discussion forum to the 'floor' either before the last pair of speakers, or after the last pair of speakers.)

Depending on your class, either let learners choose their teams and topics, or use a random selection process (your own or one from the internet). Random selection can add excitement to the selection process and avoid friendship problems.

Read through the notes and explain the procedure. Make sufficient copies of PCM 2 and hand out to your class.

Divide learners into teams of three. (If you have excess learners, they can be the adjudicators. Otherwise, select adjudicators randomly for each new debate.)

Two teams are given a particular topic to debate.

Give the teams sufficient time to discuss and research their topics. By filling in the details in the worksheet, they will have a clear overview of how the topic will be argued.

The teams choose their order of speakers.

Set out seven chairs in the front of the classroom in a semi-circle. The adjudicator sits in the centre.

Model how the adjudicator will introduce the topic and each speaker. (You may have to prompt the adjudicator throughout the debate.)

As the debate proceeds, instruct the participating teams to make notes in their worksheets for later use. The adjudicator decides who wins the debate.

Give all the teams a turn to debate their topics.

Support

Questions to guide the debate research might include:

Junk food

What are the main health problems associated with junk food?
Is junk food always bad for you?
What makes junk food different from other foods?
Is it fair to ban just junk food? What other foods are unhealthy?
Should governments decide what food children should eat or should it be their parents?
What is the best way to prepare children to eat healthy diets when they are older?

School uniforms

Does uniform affect the behaviour of students?
How does wearing school uniform affect your identity?
Do all schools make students wear uniform?
Is school uniform expensive? What about compared to normal clothes?
What sorts of clothes would you wear to school if you didn't have to wear uniform?
Do you think the school should still have rules about the kinds of clothes you could wear?

Video games

Have there been any real crimes caused by video games?
How would you choose what games to ban?
If you see violence in a game every day, how would that affect how you see the world?
There's lots of violence in films, TV and even music. Are computer games any different?
Would you ban toy guns and swords?
Are there any good things that come out of playing these games?

Non-violent crime

Is the harm that non-violent criminals do to society serious enough to deserve prison?
Prison is a harsh and cruel environment, where people are deprived of their freedom. Does a crime like theft really deserve this kind of punishment?
Criminals have cost society large amounts of money, both through their crimes and then the costs of catching them and putting them on trial. Should they not pay society back through hard work?
Could community service teach criminals valuable skills that they could then use to benefit society and themselves?

Weekly review

Level	Reading	Writing	Listening and speaking
■	Learner has great difficulty in expressing his/her thoughts clearly. Insufficient thought put into the interpretation of questions and texts. Learner has not made sufficient progress in changing one word class to another.	Learner has not been able to summarise a text satisfactorily.	Learner was not successful in arguing a topic.
●	Learner has engaged quite well with the text. Comprehension answers show a good understanding of the text. Learner has made satisfactory progress in changing one word class into another. Satisfactory spelling of words ending in –ance.	Learner has been able to engage with this skill positively.	Learner was generally able to present his/her opinions convincingly and made an attempt to engage with the opposing team's rebuttals.
▲	Learner has shown a mature understanding of the text. Answers are clearly expressed. Learner is an accurate speller and can easily switch words from one word class to another.	Learner is able to summarise texts in his/her own words using the required number of words.	Learner was able to present his/her opinions clearly and convincingly. Learner was able to engage with the opposing team's rebuttals convincingly.

Week 2

Student's Book pages 7–10

Workbook pages 4–5

Student's Book pages 7–8
Listening and speaking

1 As an introduction to the new text, discuss the questions about school outings.

2 Read the text to the class or play the digital version. Make sure that they are actively listening to you as you read.

3 It is important that learners begin to recognise and evaluate the conventions of different genres and text structures, as well as be able to compare them across a range of texts. Learners should also be guided to become more pro-active about their reading choices.

Answers
3
a Similarities: school trip, school children, history, teachers mentioned
Differences: protagonists are different genders, setting of time travel, chapter vs extracts etc.
b She could feel her tears welling up <u>again</u>.
c Short story – fewer words, more likely to take place during a constricted time period such as one day, usually have fewer characters and no subplots. A short story has much less time to hook the reader and make an impact. It must also start faster. Pacing and resolution generally must be snappy, and there is less back story in a short story.
d Open question.
e Open question.

Student's Book page 9
Comprehension

Learners complete the activity on their own.

Answers
a A museum/British Museum
b Artefacts from the ruins of Pompeii
c To guide their learning/focus their learning
d Most people forgot about filling them in and ticking off boxes
e Open question.
f Carly was clearly disinterested in the exhibition. She rather wanted to be in Oxford Street than looking at dead people in a stuffy museum.
g She was planning to find the nearest shops to visit.
h Lena did not care that Carly would get into trouble if Miss Quigley found out what she was planning to do. We read that Lena feels it's not her business anymore, showing that they must have been friends at one time.
i "Seeing them gave her a strange feeling. Perhaps these things had belonged to a girl like her."
j Open question. (The volcanic eruption)

Student's Book page 9
Writing

Discuss the structure of a dialogue. You may even wish to model the structure on the board and compare them to the original direct speech in the extract.

SANDY: Ooh, look at that! Two-thousand-year-old figs!

GARY: That loaf looks like one of my mum's cakes.

Let learners brainstorm what they could talk about in their respective dialogues.(describing and discussing the exhibits/talking to Miss Quigley/planning to sneak away)

Learners could peer-assess each other's dialogues using the rubric below.

	Yes	No
The dialogue was convincing and realistic.		
The conversation followed a logical path. I could understand it.		
I could hear clearly.		
The characters were convincing and believable.		

Student's Book page 10
Grammar

1 Choose learners at random to mime actions such as eating an apple, drinking from a glass, or writing in a book. Once the actions have been guessed, explain that the actions could be called verbs – action verbs.

Let learners complete the activity individually.

Answers
1
Mount Vesuvius, a volcano near the Bay of Naples in Italy, is hundreds of thousands of years old and has <u>erupted</u> more than 50 times. The most famous took place on the morning of 24 August, 79CE. It lasted for more than 24 hours.

Those who fled immediately had a chance of survival, but for those who stayed behind, conditions soon <u>grew</u> unbearable. As more and more ash fell, it <u>clogged</u> the air, making it almost impossible to breathe. Buildings <u>collapsed</u>. Then, a 'pyroclastic surge' (a 160-km-per-hour surge of superheated poison gas and crushed rock <u>poured</u> down the side of the mountain and <u>devoured</u> everything and everyone in its path.

By the time the Vesuvius eruption <u>sputtered</u> to an end the next day, Pompeii was buried under millions of tons of volcanic ash. About 2000 people were dead. Some people <u>drifted</u> back to town in search of lost relatives or belongings, but there was not much left to find. Pompeii, along with the smaller neighbouring towns, was no more.

Workbook page 4

Grammar

Answers
1
How to build a kite – Fly, tie
The History of Pompeii – Destroy, burn
The Alien Invasion – Fly, invade
The Stallion – Race, eat
Cooking is fun! – Burn, eat
2
a Miss Quigley <u>handed out</u> clipboards.
b Everyone <u>looked</u> at the exhibits.
c Lena <u>wanders</u> around on her own.
d Carly will <u>check</u> her phone.
e Lena <u>enjoyed</u> the exhibition.
f The room had been <u>painted</u> beautifully.
g She <u>saw</u> a girl in the reflection of the mirror.

Workbook page 5

Writing

3 Learners' own answers.

Support

Show how verbs change tense by drawing a time line

Give learners a selection of verbs to plot on the timeline.

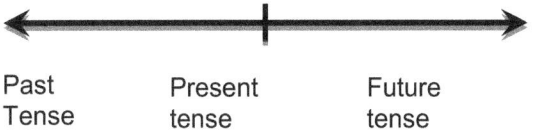

Past Tense   Present tense   Future tense

Extension

Make an alphabet list of action verbs

Let learners work out how to make a timeline for continuous verbs.

Play the verb/noun game:
- Ask learners for a list of nouns and then a second list of verbs.
- Learners then create sentences using the words in the sequence in which they have been listed. Watch how creative your learners become!

Student's Book page 10

Active and passive voice

Read through the notes on active and passive voice with the class. Check that they understand the difference between these forms.

Answers
1 erupted; grew; clogged; collapsed; poured; devoured; sputtered; drifted
2
a The people watched the volcano.
b Superhot ash smothered the town.
c Pliny wrote a diary describing the eruption.
3
a That diary must be read by you.
b The rules must be obeyed!
c This work must be redone!

Workbook page 5

Grammar

Answers
A The worksheet will be completed by Miguel
B The letter will be written by Sarah.
C I was helped by the salesman.
D The pies were baked by my mother.
E The fire was extinguished by the brave man.
F The exhibition was organised by the curator.
G The girls ignored Lena.

Weekly review

Level	Reading	Writing	Listening and speaking
■	Learner has struggled to interpret comprehension questions. Learner has a poor understanding of verbs. This has had a negative impact on his/her understanding of active and passive voice.	Learner struggled to write a sensible dialogue.	Learner does not easily contribute to class discussions. Learner found it difficult to focus whilst a text was being read aloud.
●	Learner has a satisfactory understanding of the text, and has been able to make some connections with other texts. Learner has a good understanding of active verbs, and has also a satisfactory understanding of active and passive voice.	Learner wrote a good dialogue and has shown a good understanding of this type of text.	Learner generally contributes to class discussions. Learner was able to listen actively whist a text was being read aloud.
▲	Learner has engaged fully with the extract and has interpreted the nuances of the text accurately. Learner has a mature insight and understanding. Learner has an excellent understanding of active verbs as well as an intuitive understanding of linking verbs. Learner fully understands the difference between active and passive voice.	Learner has displayed a full understanding of writing a dialogue. The conversation flowed well and realistically. Excellent characterisation.	Learner engages actively in class discussions and is able to make him/herself clearly understood. Learner listened actively to a text being read aloud and was able to remember most of what he/she had heard.

Week 3

Student's Book pages 11–14

Workbook pages 6–7

Student's Book page 11

Reading and speaking

1 Let learners read though the text on their own.

Discuss the structure of the text, drawing learners' attention to the use of headings and labelled diagrams. Also discuss the writing style.

Workbook pages 6–7

Vocabulary

Ask learners to complete the word search on their own before completing activity 2. Answers will vary.

Student's Book page 12

Comprehension

Answers
1
a The first two texts are narratives. The plot 'travels' over time. There are characters. The third text has sub-headings, photographs with captions and labelled drawings. The information is factual and non-chronological.
b The text is presenting information in a logical way.
c The language is formal as it is presenting facts. It is unemotional.
d (Learners' own opinions)
2
a Pacific Ocean – 'the ring of fire'
b A region where some of the Earth's plates meet, causing volcanoes as they collide.
c Lava – molten rock on the surface of the Earth
Magma – molten rock inside the volcano
d Open question. The greater the pressure underground, the greater the explosion.
e Volcanic ash and rock are rich in minerals and produce some of the most fertile soil in the world.

f Open question.
g Open question.
h Open question.
i To prevent loss of life
j Open question.

Student's Book page 13

Grammar

Discuss the importance of punctuation. Revise the use of full stops, exclamation marks and question marks. Also revise the use of commas. Show how the dash can replace the comma at times.

Answers
1
a Watch out – the aliens have landed!
b The images – captured by Voyager 2 – show that there are volcanoes on Jupiter's moon.
c I looked up – a ball of flames was rushing towards me!
2
a Have you ever seen an alien?
b The astronaut, on a mission to Mars, was doing experiments for NASA.
OR
The astronaut on a mission to Mars was doing experiments for NASA.
c Space travel is exciting. It is also dangerous!
OR
Space travel is exciting; it is also dangerous!

Workbook page 7

Grammar

Answers
a The volcano erupted; lava sprayed out of the crater.
OR
The volcano erupted – lava sprayed out of the crater.
b Run!
c Volcanoes are active dormant or extinct.
d Every year, all over the world, thousands of volcanoes erupt! (or full stop)
e I had never been interested in learning about volcanoes – until I saw one.
f Volcanoes have erupted in the following places: Russia, Chile and Japan.
g The journalist's report was interesting to read. (Could also be journalists')
h "Have you seen the carbonised foodstuffs?" asked Josie Dalton.

Student's Book pages 13–14

Reading and writing

Bring a selection of newspaper articles to the class. Divide learners into groups and ask them to analyse the structure of the articles. Guide them to notice the different sized headings, photographs, by-lines etc.

Ask them what differences they notice between the text on volcanoes and a newspaper report.

1 Refer learners to page 13 of the Student's Book. Examine the inverted pyramid. Discuss the structure of a newspaper report again. Discuss why reports could possibly have to be shortened (space availability).

2 Study the example of a newspaper report on page 14 of the Student's Book.

3 Instruct learners to write their own report.

Weekly review

Level	Reading	Writing
■	Learner struggles to compare writing styles and structures.	Learner has not understood the structure of a newspaper report. Learner has very little understanding of the role of punctuation in writing.
●	Learner can generally see the differences in texts and is beginning to understand that the purpose of a text affects its structure.	Learner has attempted to apply the structure of a newspaper article. Learner is showing a good understanding of the role of punctuation in writing.
▲	Learner has an excellent understanding of text structures and purposes.	Learner has shown full understanding of the structure and layout of a newspaper article. Learner shows an intuitive understanding of the role of punctuation in writing.

Unit 2 Family matters

Unit overview

The focus of this unit is family dynamics and stereotyping. Learners will have the opportunity to explore unconventional family situations through studying three different text genres. The first text is a play in which the young sister, not her four older brothers, saves the family's fortunes. The second text is a light-hearted look at dysfunctional parents, described by a thirteen-year-old boy in his diary. The final text is a poem describing the antics of a rapping granny.

This unit challenges learners to create and present their own texts, as well practise reading a play, working on their characterisation skills.

Unit 2	Reading	Writing	Listening and speaking
Family matters Texts *Amparo's Journey,* fiction, playscript *Spud,* fiction, diary extract *Gran can you rap?* poem *The man in the park,* poem	6R01 Articulate personal responses to reading, with close reference to the text. 6R02 Revise different word classes. 6Rx2 Paraphrase explicit meanings based on information from more than one point in the text. 6Ri1 Consider how the author manipulates the reaction of the reader, e.g. how characters and settings are presented. 6Ri2 Look for implicit meanings, and make plausible inferences from more than one point in the text. 6Rw1 Comment on a writer's use of language, demonstrating awareness of its impact on the reader. 6Rw2 Explore proverbs, sayings and figurative expressions. 6Rw3 Analyse the success of writing in evoking particular moods, e.g. suspense. 6Rw4 Begin to show awareness of the impact of a writer's choices of sentence length and structure. 6Rw6 Discuss and express preferences in terms of language, style and themes.	6W01 Continue to learn words, apply patterns and improve accuracy in spelling. 6Wa1 Establish and maintain a clear viewpoint, with some elaboration of personal voice. 6Wa2 Develop some imaginative detail through careful use of vocabulary and style. 6Wa3 Explore definitions and shades of meaning and use new words in context. 6Wa4 Use the styles and conventions of journalism to write reports on events. 6Wa7 Adapt the conventions of the text type for a particular purpose. 6Wa12 Use different genres as models for writing. 6Ws1 Learn word endings with different spellings but the same pronunciation, e.g. –tion, –cian, –sion, –ssion; –ance, –ence.	6SL1 Express and explain ideas clearly, making meaning explicit and respond to guidance about, and feedback on, the quality of contributions. 6SL3 Vary vocabulary, expression and tone of voice to engage the listener and suit the audience, purpose and context. 6SL5 Speak confidently in formal and informal contexts. 6SL6 Pay close attention in discussion to what others say, asking and answering questions to introduce new ideas. 6SL8 Prepare, practise and improve a spoken presentation or performance. 6SL9 Convey ideas about characters in drama in different roles and scenarios through deliberate choice of speech, gesture and movement.

	6Rw9 Read and interpret poems in which meanings are implied or multilayered.		
	6Rw10 Explore how poets manipulate and play with words and their sounds.		
	6Rw13 Identify uses of brackets.		

Related resources

- Audio files: *Amparo's Journey*; *Spud*; *Gran can you rap?*
- PCM 3: San Columbo Times
- PCM 4: Role play checklist and assessment criteria
- PCM 5: Character description

Week 1

Student's Book pages 15–18

Workbook pages 8–9

Introducing the unit

Ask learners which type of entertainment they prefer most: the stage, the big screen or television. You could do this through the medium of a Backchannel. This is a digital conversation which runs concurrently with a face-to-face conversation which gives every learner the opportunity to 'have a voice'. More information about the use and value of Backchannels can be found on the internet. (See for example http://bit.ly/1m8FfwM.)

Then ask which shows learners find most appealing, and why. Finally, ask learners to evaluate the so-called realism of digital life – families, career options, consequences of actions etc.

Student's Book pages 15–17

Listening and speaking

Ask learners about heroes and heroines in literature. Ask for the characteristics of traditional heroes and heroines. (Explain that these are called character traits.) Explain that these qualities are stereotypical and that learners will be reading a play that challenges this. Then let learners discuss the questions in small groups.

Answers

a The person most responsible for securing the safety and well-being of a family. It would be valuable to touch on how family structures in this century have challenged this.
b aunts, uncles, cousins etc.
c Divorce, HIV-AIDS, genocide have affected traditional, conventional family units.
d Open question

Reading and listening

Read the play aloud or play the audiofile. Instruct learners to listen to the play and to then discuss the questions about it in pairs. If necessary, discuss the questions as a class instead.

Comprehension

Answers
a A little village of San Colombo at the foot of the great mountains known as the Pyrenees.
b She had long straight hair as black and shiny as a raven's feathers. Her eyes were dark and blue with thick lashes and her skin was a soft brown.
c She had a terrible temper and a very stubborn streak. She was as stubborn and awkward as all the donkeys put in the village put together!
d We would expect an ordinary girl to be self-controlled and agreeable. We would not expect her to be wilful or domineering. We expect this because girls are stereotypically brought up to be more subservient than boys.
e Don Riccardo, El Fanatico. (Sentence must show an understanding of the character being a typical 'rich man or bandit'.
f Had Amparo listened to her brothers' objections to her crossing the mountain, she would never have spoken to her uncle. If she had obeyed her uncle, she would never have challenged the bandit. By being aggressive and stubborn, she solved the family's problems.
g The lynx speaks to Amparo.
h No – there would have been no proof that Amparo is so aggressive and stubborn. This makes her characters actions more believable.
i Open question.

Workbook page 8
Vocabulary

Answers
1

acting	performing the role of an imagined character
ad-lib	to make up dialogue as you go along
apron	the area of the stage that extends towards the audience
blocking	the movements of the characters decided upon by the director
character	an actor playing the role of someone else i
choreography	dance moves on stage
dialogue	conversation between characters
diction	how clearly words are spoken
flats	canvas or wood covered frames that are used for the walls of a stage setting

monologue	a speech where a character reveals personal thoughts
narrator	a character who tells the story directly to the audience
script	the text of the play
set	all the scenery that makes up the physical environment of the play
plot	the story being acted out

2
aarrrotn – narrator
eesrenyp – Pyrenees
rapmao – Amparo
aiordny – ordinary
diilv – livid
tnumoina – mountain
satseep – pesetas
terlubgiflh – bullfighter
stidanb – bandits

Student's Book page 17
Reading
Discuss the tips for presenting work to an audience. You may even ask some learners how *not* to present work as a starting point for a discussion! Let learners attempt some accents. Focus on maintaining the accent throughout the play reading. Let the groups practise reading the play and then give them the opportunity to present their work to the rest of the class. It would be valuable if you let learners assess each other's work – this reinforces the skills being developed.

Spelling
A great way to engage learners with spelling is through playing games. There are numerous apps that can be downloaded for this, including free sites that allow teachers to create their own spelling lists which can then be accessed in various games by learners.

Answers
incidence confidence subsidence evidence
influence consequence

Student's Book page 18
Punctuation
A fun way to teach learners how to punctuate sentences with brackets is to use balloons. Write the following parts of a sentence on flashcards:

The boy chased the chicken.

Write the following words on an inflated balloon: shouting loudly.

Display the flashcards and show that the balloon can be inserted between them. Then deflate the balloon to show that the sentence still makes sense. Explain that round brackets are used to show extra information and are also called parentheses.

Answers
a Amparo (a young Spanish girl) lived in the little village of San Colombo.
b El Fanatico (the cruellest bandit of all Spain) demanded money from the villagers.
c Amparo (now an old lady) still lives with her brothers in the little village.

Support
Give your weaker learners a few balloons and let them create their own sentences, modelling their sentences on those in Student's Book.

Student's Book page 18
Grammar
Read through the notes on adverbs. Make sure that learners understand that an adverb can be a single word or a phrase, and that adverbs modify verbs, adjectives and other adverbs.

Workbook page 9

Grammar

Answers
a I went to a show yesterday.
b Maya left her programme on the counter.
c The usher guided us to our seats.
d We'll buy popcorn during interval.
e We'll have to be quiet during the performance.
f The first act will start just now.
g The rehearsals went smoothly.
h The audience applauded enthusiastically!
i The lead spoke her lines too softly at times.
j We impatiently waited for the curtains to open.
k There'll be another performance tonight.
l The review of the show will be in the paper tomorrow morning.
m Our car is parked around the corner.
n I'm so glad I bought tickets this afternoon.

Student's Book page 18

Punctuation

Refer learners to the word cloud and instruct them to create sentences of their own. Examples of sentences:

1. The birds sang <u>sweetly</u>.

2. The family sat in the <u>garden</u>.

3. The old man walked <u>rather slowly in the garden</u>.

Extension

Let learners make a list of adverbs and present this as a word cloud. There is a free app called 'Wordificator' which could be used.

Student's Book page 18

Writing

It is important that learners can adapt texts from one format to another. As diary writing is very simple, tell learners that they will be writing Amparo's next adventure in the form of a newspaper article. This will revise the skills acquired in Unit 1. Give each learner a copy of PCM 3 to use for their final draft.

Weekly review

Level	Reading	Writing	Listening and speaking
■	Insufficient evidence of understanding of the text. Learner does not recognise or understand stereotypes in literature.	Learner's newspaper article lacked content and was poorly structured. Learner needs much more practise with recognising and using adverbs. Poor understanding of round brackets.	Learner has not engaged with the task. Poor pronunciation and weak phrasing. Learner has not connected with fellow readers or the audience.
●	Learner has shown a good understanding of the text. S/he is beginning to grasp the implications of stereotypes in literature.	Learner was able to write a satisfactory newspaper report about a character's experience. Learner has shown a satisfactory understanding of adverbs. Good understanding of round brackets.	Learner participated actively in the play reading. An attempt was made to stay in character. Satisfactory pausing, eye contact and interaction with fellow readers and audience.
▲	Learner has shown an excellent understanding of the text and has a satisfactory grasp of how characters can be stereotypes.	Learner was able to write an original and entertaining adventure as a newspaper article. Learner is consistently able to recognise adverbs correctly. Excellent understanding of the function of round brackets.	Learner has an instinctive 'feel' for creating a character when reading aloud. Excellent pausing, eye contact and interaction with fellow readers and audience.

Week 2

Student's Book pages 19–22

Workbook pages 10–11

Student's Book pages 19–20

Speaking and reading

1 Introduce the new text by discussing television shows or books learners have read that feature families. Then refer learners to the questions preceding the extract of 'Spud' by John van de Ruit. These should generate a lively discussion.

Read the back cover blurb to the class before moving onto the diary extract. Spud has been made into a film that received quite a lot of acclaim, so learners may be familiar with the story.

2 Depending on the ability level of your class, either let learners read the text themselves, or read it to them. Alternatively, let learners listen to the audiofile of the extract.

Answers
3
a Woke up at 4.30 am. Heart beating like a bongo drum.
b Learner's Open question. (The exaggeration draws the reader into the story. Turns ordinary events into unrealistic, yet believable, actions.)
c Dad fires up his supersonic heat-seeking rose sprayer, wearing only his Cricketing Legends sleeping shorts and a surgeon's mask, to protect himself from the deadly chemicals that he's spraying into the atmosphere and dances like a loon.
d Most likely the neighbours – He's always threatening to sue them or thrash them within an inch of their lives. This shows that there is a very poor relationship between them.
e Police are supposed to be brave protectors, not weak cowards running away from a woman dressed in a yellowy green night gown.
f The word 'anyway' shows us that Spud would have battled to eat the eggs had he been nervous or not.
g Open question.
h Open question.
i Yes. He seems to be the adult in the family and can therefore manage the new experiences he will face.

Student's Book page 21

Writing and speaking

1 Discuss the structure of the extract. Compare the structure to that of a newspaper article as well as to that of a play script. Revise the structure of a script and, if necessary, refer to 'Amparo's Journey' on page 15 of the Student's Book. Divide learners into groups of three. Instruct them to rewrite the extract taken from 'Spud' by John van de Ruit as a playscript. Give the groups enough time to practise their lines as they will be required to read their scripts in front of the class. Stress that they do not have to learn their lines, but must focus on characterisation, and audience connection. To develop their understanding of the assessment procedure, give learners copies of PCM 4 to complete as a peer assessment.

Workbook page 10

Reading and thinking

Answers

Amparo: bad-tempered, stubborn, mature; El Fanatico: childish; cruel; Uncle Carlos: cowardly, kind, caring; Spud: nervous; Spud's father: eccentric; Spud's mother: intimidating

Workbook page 10

Vocabulary

5

CHARACTER TRAIT	SYNONYM	ANTONYM
kind	caring	unkind
cowardly	frightened	brave
childish	immature	mature
eccentric	strange	predictable
intimidating	threatening	friendly
nervous	worried	calm
cruel	harsh	kind
stubborn	determined	flexible
bad-tempered	irritable	friendly
caring	loving	cruel

Student's Book page 21

Writing and speaking

2 Instruct learners to work in pairs. They are to choose one of the scenarios and role play the scene. It is important that the scene be fully planned and practised before being performed. To add even more fun to the activity, allow learners to dress the part.

Give each learner/pair a copy of PCM 4: Role play checklist and assessment criteria. The assessment criteria will help focus learners' attention during the performances.

Student's Book page 21

Writing and speaking

4 Discuss the humour of the extract. Explore the use of exaggeration as a tool to create humour. Bear in mind that humour is very subjective and that some learners may not find this type of story funny at all.

Give each learner a copy of PCM 5: Character description

Answers

3

Character	Information about the character	Proof from text
Spud	• Is nervous about going to boarding school. • Is disrespectful towards grandmother • Is embarrassed by parents • He is resourceful	'…my heart is beating like a bongo drum' '…blew Wombat's…' '…Maybe boarding school…' '…I would have thrown…'
Mr Milton	• Eccentric • Doesn't care what other people think • Can't be taken seriously	'…Dad fires up his supersonic…' '…wearing only his Cricketing Legends sleeping shorts…' '…dances like a loon…'
Mrs Milton	• The stronger parent • aggressive • not a typical mother	'…mother stalks into the garden…' '…my mother verbally abuses the policemen' '…Mom's notorious for her dreadful cooking…'

Workbook page 11

Grammar

This activity will develop learners' understanding of how adverbs can add colour and depth to their writing.

Answers
The kitten <u>purrs</u> *gently*.
The clock ticks *patiently*.
The toaster pops *cheekily*.
The frying pan hisses *warningly*.
The drain gurgles *rudely*.
The baby cries *all day long*.
The chair squeaks *irritatingly*.
The curtain swishes *haughtily*.
The stair creaks *painfully*.

Student's Book page 22

Reading and speaking

1 If possible, play an audiofile of a wild wind. There are many free recordings available. Give random learners an opportunity to describe what they hear. As they do so, write the adjectives and adverbs on the board.

Then discuss the sentence about the wind:

The sulking wind blew listlessly, picking up scraps of paper and them throwing them down just as quickly.

Answers
a We can tell that the wind is not strong as we read that it blows listlessly which shows that it is weak and disinterested.
b The verbs in the sentence are too weak to capture the energy of a storm.
c Description of a hot summer's day
d Learners' own sentences

Ask learners to share the sentences they have written with the class.

2 Instruct learners to study and think about the photograph. Encourage learners to brainstorm words that could be used in their sentences by organising their thoughts using a mind map. Encourage your stronger learners to use figurative language.

Weekly review

Level	Reading	Writing	Listening and speaking
■	Learner has a poor understanding of how humour is created through exaggeration.	Learner struggled to rewrite the diary as a narrated dialogue. Main points of the plot were excluded. Learner is not able to use adjectives and adverbs to create images effectively.	Role play was poorly executed. Characterisation was poor and unrealistic.
●	Learner has a fairly good understanding of how words can be manipulated to create humorous mood.	Learner was able to change the text style fairly well. Learner is attempting to use adjectives and adverbs to create interesting imagery.	A pleasing role play. The storyline was believable and an effort was made to create a realistic character.
▲	Learner has a very clear understanding of how words can be manipulated to create mood.	Learner was able to effectively rewrite the diary in the form of a narrated dialogue. Learner has a strong sense of imagery and is able to communicate these ideas effectively.	Role play was well-planned and very well executed. Excellent characterisation.

Week 3

Student's Book pages 23–26

Workbook pages 12–13

If possible, begin the lesson by showing a video of Benjamin Zephaniah reciting one of his poems. Alternatively, play a video of Michael Rosen rapping one of his poems. You can find many examples online, and www.poetryarchive.org has biographical information and work from a range of established poets. For example, your class might be interested to learn that Benjamin Zephaniah left school at 13 unable to read or write properly and that he ended up in prison for burglary. His anger stayed with him, but now it is channelled into protest, music and performance.

Discuss the power of words and how music and poetry can inspire generations.

Student's Book pages 23–24

Listening and writing

Discuss the introductory questions. It is important that learners are able to identify and understand the different types of rhymes they will come across in the rap poem. Internal rhyme is a strong element of rap.

Write the first line from Edgar Allan Poe's poem, 'The Raven' on the board:

> *Once upon a midnight **dreary**, while I pondered, weak and **weary**.*

Guide learners to identify the rhyming and placement of the bold words. This is called internal rhyming.

1 Play the recording of 'Gran, can you rap?' by Jack Ousbey or read it aloud. Instruct learners to 'feel' the rhythm in the words and to tap the beat out as you read.

Workbook page 12

Reading and writing

Answers
1
Single syllable words: rap, beat
Two syllable words: trumpet, rhyming, poet, raucous, jarring, chorus
Three syllable words: musician, poetry, monotone, syllables, resonant, melodic, simile
Four syllable words: cacophony
2
Rhyming words
Earth, mirth
Strange, range
Trouble, double
Toffee, coffee
Jump, thump
Height, kite
Carrot, parrot
Chatter, clatter
Stony, lonely
Empower, hour
Water, daughter
Learners write their own couplets

Extension
Challenge learners to include internal rhyming in their couplets as well.

Student's Book pages 24–25
Listening and writing
2 After listening to the poem, let learners discuss, and then write, the answers to the comprehension questions.

Answers
a We do not expect grannies to rap and dance around.
b Grannies stereotypically are expected to knit, babysit, gossip etc
c Open question
d By choosing an unusual situation – a granny rapping!
e To symbolise the informality and lack of regularity in the structure of rap poetry
f Raps are meant to be free flowing, to reflect the break with formality and confining conventions.
g The Shel Silverstein poem has a structured rhythm and rhyming scheme. It also has rhyming couplets.
h Open question.

Workbook page 13
Reading and writing

Answers

Assonance in verse 1: rose, rolled, rolled and rolled; in, bim, nip and yip; rap, bam, rapping, nap, yap, rap and rap; room and boom; head and said; seen and queen.

End rhymes in verse 3: street and feet; red and said; seen and queen.

Alliteration in final verse: she, she, she, she and slip-slap; rapped, rapped, rapping, rapping, rap-rap; rapping and rap-rap; Gran's, Gran and Gran; tip-top; trip-trap; slip-slap; nip-nap; yip-yap; hip-hop; touch yer cap and take a nap; happy, happy, happy and happy.

Student's Book pages 25–26
Speaking and writing
1 Divide learners into small groups. Give each group one verse to learn. Let the groups stand together and then perform their respective verses in chronological order. If possible, video or record the performance and show it to your class.

Extension
Let learners record themselves using an app such as Soundcloud.

2 Discuss the role emoticons play in texting. Let learners complete the activity.

Answers
a I have no idea!
b You're looking for trouble…
c Your secret is safe with me!
d I'm not interested! Leave me out of it!
e Just leave me alone!

Extension
Learners can create their own set of emoticons according to a theme, for example cat faces, flowers, insects.

3 Learners write their own sentences for each emoji.

4 Learners write sentences to describe the rapping granny.

Support
Give learners prompts to guide their writing, such as:

- The granny's voice is as loud as _____. She loves rapping even though she sounds like a _____. She dresses very strangely. Her jersey is as red as _____ and her skirt is as blue as _____. Granny's face is as wrinkled as _____.

- Once learners have a better understanding of the task, give them key words to use in sentences. Stress that not every sentence has to include a simile.

- It could be helpful to find a picture of a granny for learners to describe.

Extension
- Let learners use adjectival and adverbial phrases to expand their descriptions in a meaningful way.
- Learners could create a 'Wanted poster' describing the granny. (There are apps and website tools which can offer templates for this.)
- Let learners write and perform their own rap.

Student's Book page 26

Reading and speaking

Answers
When in Rome, do as the Romans do – Fit in with the people around you
When the going gets tough, the tough get going – Don't let challenges beat you
You can't judge a book by its cover – Don't judge people with preconceived ideas
Better late than never – It's never too late to try something new
Actions speak louder than words – What you do is more important than what you say.
If you can't beat 'em, join 'em – Sometimes it's easier to conform than to stand out.

Extension
- Divide learners into small groups. Give each group a proverb. The group must mime a scenario to describe the meaning of the proverb.
- Let learners research proverbs and choose five to reflect a theme of their own choice.

Weekly review

Level	Reading	Writing	Speaking
■	Learner is not able to identify internal and external rhyming. Weak understanding of alliteration. Poor understanding of syllables.	Learner needs more support in using similes to expand sentences sensibly.	Learner has not been able to express the rap rhythmically. The essence of rapping has not been communicated.
●	Learner generally understands the impact of rhyming words in rap poetry. Good use of syllables and alliteration.	Learner uses similes to expand sentences although the images are rather clichéd.	Learner generally understands the characteristics of rapping and has presented the rap well.
▲	Learner has an excellent understanding of the elements of raps: rhyme, rhythm, alliteration, syllables.	Learner is able to create fresh, original similes to create descriptions of characters.	Learner is able to rap with an appropriate beat. The presentation is entertaining.

Unit 3 From pencils to pixels

Unit overview

As learners work through this unit they will explore how education has changed over the years. They will examine and analyse different texts that have been written in different styles and will eventually write an imaginary autobiography. The emphasis of this chapter is on the analysis of the texts' characteristics, with an additional focus on inferential interpretation of content. The influence of the narrator's voice will also be explored.

Unit 3	Reading	Writing	Listening and speaking
From pencils to pixels Texts *David Copperfield,* fiction, extended narrative *Malala Yousafzai,* non-fiction, autobiography and blog *Perspective,* non-fiction formal and impersonal *The hole in the wall project,* non-fiction, biography and journalistic writing	6R01 Articulate personal responses to reading, with close reference to the text. 6R02 Revise different word classes. 6Rx1 Distinguish between fact and opinion in a range of texts and other media. 6Rx2 Paraphrase explicit meanings based on information from more than one point in the text. 6Ri1 Consider how the author manipulates the reaction of the reader, e.g. how characters and settings are presented. 6Ri2 Look for implicit meanings, and make plausible inferences from more than one point in the text. 6Rw1 Comment on a writer's use of language, demonstrating awareness of its impact on the reader. 6Rw5 Understand the use of conditionals, e.g. to express possibility. 6Rw6 Discuss and express preferences in terms of language, style and themes. 6Rw12 Understand changes over time in words and expressions and their use. 6Rv1 Recognise key characteristics of a range of non-fiction text types.	6W01 Continue to learn words, apply patterns and improve accuracy in spelling. 6Wa1 Establish and maintain a clear viewpoint, with some elaboration of personal voice. 6Wa3 Explore definitions and shades of meaning and use new words in context. 6Wa6 Develop skills of writing biography and autobiography in role. 6Wa7 Adapt the conventions of the text type for a particular purpose. 6Wa12 Use different genres as models for writing. 6Wp4 Develop increasing accuracy in using punctuation effectively to mark out the meaning in complex sentences. 6Wp5 Punctuate speech and use apostrophes accurately. 6Ws1 Learn word endings with different spellings but the same pronunciation, e.g. *–tion, –cian,* 6Ws6 Explore word origins and derivations and the use of words from other languages.	6SL1 Express and explain ideas clearly, making meaning explicit and respond to guidance about, and feedback on, the quality of contributions. 6SL5 Speak confidently in formal and informal contexts. 6SL6 Pay close attention in discussion to what others say, asking and answering questions to introduce new ideas. 6SL7 Help to move group discussion forward, e.g. by clarifying, summarising.

	6Rv2 Understand the conventions of standard English usage in different forms of writing.		
	6Rv3 Revise language conventions and grammatical features of different types of text.		
	6Rv4 Compare the language, style and impact of a range of non-fiction writing.		
	6Rv5 Explore autobiography and biography, and first and third person narration.		
	6Rv8 Begin to develop awareness that the context for which the writer is writing and the context in which the reader is reading can impact on how the text is understood.		

Related resources

- Audio files: *David Copperfield*; *I am Malala*; *The Whole in the Wall Project*
- PCM 6: The possessive apostrophe
- PCM 7: Collective nouns
- PCM 8: Contractions
- PCM 9: Comparison table

Introducing the unit
Use the photographs of classrooms as a stimulus for a discussion about how education has changed over time.

You could also play the Pink Floyd song 'Another brick in the wall'. Before playing it, explain that the song was written as a protest against rigid schooling in general, especially boarding schools. You could even find a YouTube video of the song being performed and show it to learners. Discuss the lyrics of the song, relating them to learners' own experiences, or those of friends and family members.

Week 1

Student's Book pages 27–30

Workbook pages 14–15

Student's Book page 27

Listening and speaking

a Ask learners what they know about Victorian England. (They did some reading about this in Stage 4). It would be helpful, for context, to use some interactive resources to introduce this section of the topic. Otherwise, source some photographs that you can project in order to generate a discussion. Make sure that learners understand the social significances of child labour. Discuss the differences between rights and responsibilities, and link these to learners' schooling situations.

Tell the class that Charles Dickens was born in 1812, the second of eight children. Unfortunately his father was a very poor businessman and, when Charles was ten, he was arrested and thrown in debtors' prison. Dickens' mother moved into the prison with seven of her children whilst Charles lived outside the prison in order to earn money for the struggling family. The family's fortunes did eventually change for the better and, in 1849, Dickens began to write *David Copperfield*, a novel which reflected his early life experiences.

b Before they begin reading, ask learners to study the picture on page 28. Ask them to predict what the text will be about. Let learners read the text independently, making notes of difficult vocabulary which can then be explained before the continuation of the lesson.

Student's Book page 28

Comprehension

Learners discuss the comprehension questions as a class.

Answers
1
a The headmaster
b A teacher's assistant/ senior pupil
c The hushed silence occurred suddenly, creating tension in the air.
d His cane breaks skin, just as a bite does. The cane causes pain.
e Discussion – guide learners to look at changing Mr Creakle's personality, and then discuss the implications of this. Alternatively, David Copperfield's personality could be changed. Encourage learners to examine the implications of any changes they suggest.
f Discussion – Most likely not, as Mr Creakle is completely authoritarian and powerful. Victorian society did not accommodate freedom of speech in children.

2 Learners discuss questions with a partner and then work independently, writing their answers in their books.

Answers
a The stepfather has no patience/unkind man/jealous of the boy.
b Both men are bullies, both dislike children.
c Copperfield is timid. He wants to please, but is too frightened to stand up for himself.
d So that they do not draw attention to themselves, thereby earning a beating, too.
e Open question. A good discussion question once the task has been completed. Discuss the shock-factor of unexpected cruelty. Discuss intentional cruelty versus unintentional cruelty.
f Open question. Guide learners to be realistic and to take the circumstances into context at all times.
g Open question. Perhaps you could answer the question in two different time settings: Victorian times and current times.
h The reader dislikes Mr Creakle because the writer describes him in such a negative way. He has no positive attributes what so ever. He is seen as a bully.

i The reader has sympathy towards Copperfield as he is shown to be a small, timid little boy who is being undeservedly cruelly treated. Although he bit his stepfather, it seems like this was in self-defence. The punishment does not fit the 'crime'.

Student's Book page 29

Vocabulary

Read through the vocabulary box of Victorian slang. Challenge learners to supply modern day slang or informally used words to replace the Victorian slang. For example, 'threads' could replace 'dunnage'.

Student's Book page 29

Listening and speaking

Challenge your learners to create a Victorian street slang dialogue to present to the class.

If possible, watch video clips some scenes from the film *Oliver* in order to put the vocabulary in context. Ask learners to watch the videos carefully and use them as inspiration for their dialogues that they will be creating.

Student's Book page 29

Grammar

Although learners will have been exposed to nouns in earlier years, they tend to forget the finer details, and it is a good idea to revise this word class.

Answers
1 Alphabetical order of common nouns (an example)
Boys, Breakfast, Captives, Day, Doorway, Elbow, Giant, School, Storybook, Voices
2
- Mr Creakle – 6 times
- Tungay – 3 times
- Steerforth – once
- Salem House – once

Workbook page 14

Grammar

Answers
The following responses are possible. Learners will have to think creatively and invent plausible proper nouns!

Common nouns	Proper nouns	Abstract nouns
Boys	Mr Creakle	Fear
Desks	David Copperfield	Sadness
Cane	Boy's name (own idea)	Cruelty
Shoes	Boy's name (own idea)	Hunger
Face	Boy's name (own idea)	Distrust
Hair	School's name (own idea)	Annoyance
Floor	Country (own idea)	Punishment

Extension
Pie Corbett has a wonderful writing game (search for it online) which would be suitable to challenge and engage your learners: ask learners to explain the collective nouns in the alphabet in PCM 7: Collective nouns and then create their own alphabet. This might best be done in small teams, dividing the alphabet up between them.

Student's Book page 30

Spelling and vocabulary

Answers
1
Pair of spectacles – optician
Man pulling a rabbit out of a hat – magician
Light switch – electrician
Music notes – musician
Children's doctor – paediatrician

2 One of the most common errors learners make is using an apostrophe to show a plural. It is essential that this be addressed in the classroom. If possible, find local examples to show incorrect usage and show these to the class. Signs in shops are often a good source of this. Alternatively, ask the class to take photographs of incorrect usage and make a class display (with corrections).

Answers
a Mr Creakle's punishments were too severe!
b David Copperfield's eyes could not stop closing.
c The three boys' books were on the table.
d Have you seen the pickpockets steal anything yet?

Workbook page 15

Spelling and punctuation

Answers

> Dear Mum and Dad
> Thank you for the parcel that you sent me. I've eaten all the biscuits and candy. My friends are quite jealous of me! They don't have any snacks to eat, so I didn't keep my treats to myself!
> Mr Creakle isn't a very kind man – he beats us when we make mistakes. I'm very scared of him. This isn't a happy school. We're all so frightened of Mr Creakle that we can't work properly.
> When are you coming to fetch me? David Copperfield's mother wants to fetch him, but his stepfather's too mean to let him go back home. Couldn't David come home with me? It'd be such fun and we'd do all the chores around the house. You're always complaining about needing more help.
> Your loving son
> Phillip

Support
The possessive apostrophe is quite challenging, so you may wish to reinforce this concept using PCM 6: The possessive apostrophe.

Extension
1 Watch the movie *Oliver!*.
2 Encourage the stronger learners to do research on children in Victorian England. They could create a digital presentation for the class.
3 Let learners read *David Copperfield* or *Oliver Twist*.

Weekly review

Level	Reading	Writing	Listening and speaking
■	Learner needs more practise in engaging on a deeper level with texts.	Learner still operates at basic level, using simple vocabulary for written expression. Poor understanding of the apostrophe. Poor execution of the autobiographical paragraph. Learner has a weak grasp of 'point of view'.	Very little participation in class and group discussions. Learner was not really able to engage with the Cockney dialogue successfully.
●	Learner has shown a good understanding of the text and is starting to interpret the nuances of words to deepen understanding.	Learner is attempting to experiment with words to express meaning and interpretation. Satisfactory autobiographical paragraph. Shows good understanding of the apostrophe.	Learner has generally participated in a positive way in class and group discussions. Cockney dialogue was well-planned.
▲	Learner has a clear understanding of the nuances of words and how they impact on the reader's interpretation and understanding.	Learner has a well-developed vocabulary and is able to express thoughts and opinions accurately. A most pleasing autobiographical paragraph – clear understanding of writing conventions is evident. Excellent punctuation skills.	Although this learner is an enthusiastic participant in group and class discussions, s/he has shown a sincere interest in the contributions of other learners and has acknowledged their opinions positively. A highly entertaining and sensible Cockney dialogue.

Week 2

Student's Book pages 33–36

Workbook pages 16–17

Introducing the unit

Before you begin this unit, create a digital presentation with each of the following quotes on a separate slide as well as a final slide consisting of a photograph of Malala Yousafzai.

You can also print these quotes separately so that they can be handed out to different groups for discussion.

- "Why shall I wait for someone else? Why shall I be looking to the government, to the army, that they would help us … for them to help me. Why don't I raise my voice? Why don't we speak up for our rights?"
- "I truly believe the only way we can create global peace is through not only educating our minds, but our hearts and our souls."
- "I think life is always dangerous. Some people get afraid of it. Some people don't go forward. But some people, if they want to achieve their goal, they have to go. They have to move …"
- "One child, one teacher, one book and one pen can change the world. Education is the only solution. Education first."
- "When the whole world is silent, even one voice becomes powerful."
- "It feels like this life is not my life. It's a second life. People have prayed to God to spare me and I was spared for a reason — to use my life for helping people."

Divide your class into groups and give each group quote to examine. Ask your learners to discuss the type of person that would have made the statements they have been given to read. Ask the groups to create a character profile of this person and let them share this with the rest of the class. As the groups do their report back, project the PowerPoint slide on a screen so that all learners can get a real sense of the words in the quote.

Show the photograph of Malala and tell the class that the quotes are from her. Now discuss the quotes again – point out any changes in perception of learners. Direct learners to page 31 of their Student's Book, and read the introduction to the reading passage as well as the biography box.

Instruct learners to write down questions they would like to ask Malala as they listen to an extract from her autobiography. (They will use these questions at a later stage.)

Student's Book page 33

Listening and speaking

Ask learners what they know about Victorian England. (They did some reading about this in Stage 4). It would be helpful, for context, to use some interactive resources to introduce this section of the topic. Otherwise, source some photographs that you can project in order to generate a discussion. Make sure that learners understand the social significances of child labour. Discuss the differences between rights and responsibilities, and link these to learners' schooling situations.

Answers

1

a An activist is someone who campaigns for some kind of social change.
b Own opinions. Responses will most likely range from learners condemning the BBC for putting a teenager in danger, to applauding the BBC for exposing the problems girls like Malala face. The focus must, however, be on Malala's role – was she brave or looking for trouble?
c Learners will again discuss their own views – their responses could well be a reflection of their own home circumstances.
d This answer will depend on their response to the previous question.

Divide learners into groups and let them share and discuss the questions they had thought of. Discuss the more interesting questions as a class.

Student's Book page 33

Comprehension

1 Divide learners into pairs. For variation, team up learners of similar ability. Answers will vary, which is exactly what you want! The important thing is that your learners are able to explain and justify their opinions and answers.

Answers

a A bookish girl is someone who enjoys reading and studying.
b Open question. Answers to include:

My life	Areas to compare	Malala's life in Pakistan
	Schooling	Hidden away from public view Not compulsory Regimented
	Transport to school	Rickshaws
	Lifestyle	Oil lamps No running water Ovens need gas fuel Shop in bazaars No ready-made meals
	Social activities	Friends movies

c Malala did not hide the fact that she no longer wished to become a doctor. Her parents knew that she preferred to become an inventor or politician.
2 We infers that school is the one place where girls have the freedom to be themselves, to be unique individuals, to dream.
3 Open question.

Student's Book page 33

Speaking

Before learners attempt this activity, discuss the difference between open and closed questions. Depending on the level of your class, you could play the following game to help your learners develop their understanding of open and closed questions:

Tell them:

I have a story that has a hidden mystery in it. Everything about the story is ordinary, except one thing. You have to ask me questions until you guess the one unusual thing. Try to imagine the entire scene. It may help if you think about questions that start with words like "who, when, or where."

Respond to their questions, gradually revealing clues. When they force you to describe the hidden mystery, they have won the game. Comment on perceptive and helpful questions as they ask them.

A closed question can be answered with either a single word or a short phrase. Closed questions have the following characteristics:
- They give you facts.
- They are easy to answer.
- They are quick to answer.
- E.g. Are you happy?

An open question is likely to receive a long answer. Open questions have the following characteristics:
- They ask the respondent to think and reflect.
- They will give you *opinions* and *feelings*.
- Open questions begin with words such as: what, why, how, describe.
- E.g. what did you do on holidays? Why is that so important to you?

Discuss the etiquette of digital communication. For example, good guidelines for learners to follow may include:
- Always make sure you follow "netiquette".
- Consider whether what you are writing is appropriate *before* you hit the submit button.
- Always be polite. It does not matter if you agree or disagree with what you are reading in a blog.
- Don't write anything you would be ashamed of saying to someone's face. Don't hurt somebody's feelings.

Workbook page 16

Writing

3 *Answers to this activity will vary.*

Student's Book page 34

Grammar

Example answers
1
a Pakistan is a **beautiful** country.
b Malala felt **honoured** to receive a prestigious award.
2
a The **Pakistani** schools are mostly for boys.
b Malala and her friend loved listening to **American** musicians such as Justin Bieber.
3
a Malala had a good relationship with **her** parents.
b The Pakistani girls took **their** education seriously.

4

Adjective	Abstract noun	Adjective	Abstract noun
peaceful	peace	loyal	loyalty
joyful	joy	miserable	misery
careful	care	brave	bravery
kind	kindness	sophisticated	sophistication
sad	sadness	adorable	adoration
happy	happiness	infatuated	infatuation

Student's Book page 35

Vocabulary

Vocabulary changes as needs arise. Read through and discuss the vocabulary that has developed due to the internet.

Answers
App – Software that performs a task
Cyberbully – Using the internet to bully someone
Emoticon – A symbol made out of punctuation marks
Hotspot – WiFi access in public places
Infomania – Constantly checking your phone
Netiquette – internet manners
Photobomb – Intrude into the background of a photo
Selfie – Taking a photo of yourself
Tweeps – People who follow you on Twitter

Extension

Let learners create their own, original vocabulary lists for digital concepts.

Student's Book pages 35–36

Reading

1 Ask learners what the following statement means: There are three sides to every story. Guide them to understand that an event can be interpreted in various ways, depending on the people involved. Explain that this is similar in writing. The author will 'show' an opinion by the way a text is written. This is called the author's voice and can be interpreted through the vocabulary the author uses. Discuss whether authors always show their perspective when they write. Authors can give their characters 'voices' depending on the point of view they are using in their writing.

Write the following sentences on the board:
The girl laughed loudly.
The girl laughed like a hyena.

Discuss how the author's voice is evident, especially in the second sentence.

Discuss the different points of view found in literature. Explain that the second person point of view is seldom seen in literature except in books such as the Goosebumps series.

Definitions of points of view

First person	Used mainly for autobiographical writing, such as a personal essay or a memoir. Pronouns such as I, my, we Academics and journalists usually avoid first person in their writing as they must be seen to be objective and distanced from the topic.
Second person	Pronouns such as: You, yours, yourself, yourselves. Used mostly in emails, letters, speeches.
Third person	A form of storytelling in which a narrator relates all action in third person, using pronouns such as "he" or "she." Third person point of view may be objective, limited or omniscient.

Workbook page 17
Writing
Explain the different ways of indicating points of view.

Divide learners into pairs. To assist weaker learners, team them up with stronger learners. Explain that they will be exploring how authors use point of view in their writing.

Student's Book page 36
Reading

Answers
2 Open question.
- David Copperfield – vocabulary is 'complicated'. Copperfield's 'inner voice' is formal, reflecting the formality of the time. Definite hierarchy.
- Malala's blog – casual and chatty. Shows no hierarchy.
- Both texts are written in the first person, from the protagonist's point of view.
- Own insight. Guide learners to see how 3rd person distances the protagonist from the plot

Student's Book page 36
Listening and speaking

Let learners discuss the questions in groups. Ensure that each learner is given the chance to give their opinion in their group.

Extension
Let learners write a section of either text from a different point of view or even a different character's perspective

Weekly review

Level	Reading	Writing	Listening and speaking
■	Learner needs more practise in engaging on a deeper level with texts. Learner has difficulty in answering and formulating open questions Learner struggles to identify different types of adjectives in texts.	Learner has very little understanding of point of view in different texts.	Very little participation in class and group discussions. Learner makes very few contributions.
●	Learner has shown a good understanding of the text and is starting to interpret the nuances of words to deepen understanding. Learner was able to ask meaningful questions to develop personal understanding. Learner is able to identify most of the adjectives in a text and is displaying an understanding of the function of this word class.	Learner is gaining confidence in identifying different points of view in texts.	Learner has generally participated in a positive way in class and group discussions.
▲	Learner has a clear understanding of the nuances of words and how they impact on the reader's interpretation and understanding. Learner is able to consistently ask insightful questions. Learner shows an intuitive understanding of this word class.	Learner shows a good grasp of points of view in texts and shows an understanding of author's voice in texts.	Learner is able to engage meaningfully with discussions around the text and shows an interest in learning more about the topic.

Week 3

Student's Book pages 37–39

Workbook pages 18–19

Student's Book page 37

Reading and speaking

Hold a class discussion. Ask learners how they think children in isolated, rural areas get an education. Discuss the varying standards of education around the world. Discuss the importance of education.

Ask for suggestions of how children in rural areas could be educated in a sustainable, significant manner.

Allow learners to discuss the preparatory questions in small groups. There should be quite lively discussions as learners have experience of the internet, and most likely have heard their parents/influential adults speak about how the internet has negatively affected education.

Draw learners' attention to the images on the page. Discuss the biographical details of Dr Sugata Mitra. Then instruct learners to examine the images and text on the next page. Ask random learners what they think the text will be about. If you have time, play his

TED talk to the class: he is an entertaining man and learners will enjoy listening to him.

Give learners time to read the text and to talk amongst themselves before moving on.

Student's Book page 38

Comprehension

Instruct learners to answer the questions independently before sharing their answers with fellow group members.

Example answers
a No, children can be taught by anyone, anywhere. (Guide learners to reflect critically on the mind map and to evaluate its content.)
b If children in those rural areas can learn new skills and content by working independently, having to use their own intuition, then established schools are not serving their purpose of being institutions of learning, growth and development. Children in urban areas should be learning far more, and doing far more, given the resources and opportunities they enjoy.
c This is a metaphor, comparing the learning station to a well. A well provides water, which we need for survival and development. Similarly, the learning station gives children the means to gain the knowledge they need for growth and development.
d
Vision – dream
Embedded – fixed
Theory – belief
Employs – adopts
Broaden – develops
e Open question

Student's Book pages 38–39

Spelling and vocabulary

1 Remind learners about nouns which end in the *shun* sound and talk about how to spell them before completing the activity.

Answers

educate	educa**tion**	protect	protec**tion**
facilitate	facilita**tion**	detect	detec**tion**
dominate	domina**tion**	reject	rejec**tion**
renovate	renova**tion**	inflect	inflec**tion**
part	parti**tion**	describe	descrip**tion**
add	addi**tion**	prescribe	prescrip**tion**
consider	considera**tion**	satisfy	satisfac**tion**
register	registra**tion**	multiply	multiplica**tion**

2 Revise the use of the apostrophe to show possession. Then show how the apostrophe is also used for contractions. Emphasise that the apostrophe replaces the missing words.

Answers
a Children <u>don't</u> always need adults to teach them.
b It <u>isn't</u> easy for children in rural areas to receive a good education.
c Sugata Mitra <u>wouldn't</u> give up on his dream.
d The children in the slums <u>could've</u> ignored the computer in the wall, but they didn't.

Support

Hand out copies of PCM 8: Contractions.

Answers
1 The bird stretched its wings.
2 He's going to play football this afternoon.
3 It's a beautiful day.
4 Adam is looking for his pen.
5 My friend found his book on the floor.
6 You're responsible for your own property.
7 My neighbour say he's going to paint his house.
8 It's interesting to watch a lion catch its prey.
9 – 15 Open question.

Student's Book page 39

Thinking deeper

Talk about how the internet has turned the world into a global village, making physical boundaries less and less of an obstacle to the spread of information. Discuss the impact this will have on the 'blending' of vocabulary.

Answers
- khaki – Hindi, denim – French, zombie, West African via the Caribbean, tomato – Aztec/Mexican, magazine – Arabic
- Learners' own research.

Extension

Let learners research the geographical origins of more words. Give learners an outline of a world map. Instruct learners to fill in 'borrowed' words in their continent of origin.

This website is useful:

http://www.collinsdictionary.com/words-and-language/word-origins/

Student's Book page 39

Speaking

Draw learners' attention to the three texts in this chapter. Discuss the structure of the texts. Allow learners to share their opinions freely.

Workbook page 18
Reading and writing
It will be easier for learners to first tabulate their findings. And to facilitate this, hand out copies of PCM 9: Comparison table. There are three activities for learners to do. Let all learners complete the first two, and leave the last one as an extension task.

Possible answers for PCM 10: Comparison table

Similarities	David Copperfield	Malala's Blog	The hole in the wall project
Content	School setting	A girl's dream for an education	Explanation of Sugata Mitra's dream of education in rural areas
Point of view	1st person	1st person	
Differences	**David Copperfield**	**Malala's Blog**	**The hole in the wall project**
Vocab	Formal, old fashioned	Modern Casual, chatty	Formal Business-like
Text characteristics	Narrative	Autobiography	Formal
Content	Story about a frightened schoolboy being bullied by a headmaster	Story about a young girl's determination to get an education for herself and others	Explanation of the way to empower rural students to become educated

Support
Help the weaker learners by filling in some of the information in the table for them before they attempt the task. Alternatively, learners could team up with a more capable learner.

Workbook page 19
Writing
Hold a class discussion about heroes and role models. Ask learners, chosen at random, who they would most like to be like. Tell learners that they are going to pretend to be someone else.

Let learners complete the table.

Student's Book page 39
Writing
Let learners use a check list like the one below to help them plan and write the autobiographical paragraph.

Structure	Topic sentence is clear and interesting. Information is sensibly and logically structured. Ideas flow well.
Content	The account is a clear account of a character, giving excellent insight into the character. The character is believable and real.
Writing style	First person Excellent use of anecdotal style of writing makes the account very personal.

Support
Help the weaker learners by filling in some of the information in the table with them.

Weekly review

Level	Reading	Writing	Listening and speaking
■	Learner needs more practise in engaging on a deeper level with texts. Learner struggles to change verbs into abstract nouns. Poor choice of synonyms show a weak understanding of the text.	Learner shows very little understanding of the conventions of autobiographical texts.	Very little participation in class and group discussions. Learner makes very few contributions.
●	Learner is developing an understanding of content shown graphically. Learner is able to change verbs into nouns with only the occasional error. Good choice of synonyms shows an understanding of the text.	Learner has written a satisfactory autobiographical account.	Learner has generally participated in a positive way in class and group discussions.
▲	Learner is able to interpret graphics accurately. Learner is able to reason logically. Learner shows an excellent command of language through the synonyms chosen. Learner can accurately apply spelling rules to change verbs to nouns.	Learner's autobiographical account is sincerely written. Lovely use of anecdotes makes the text real and interesting to read.	Learner is able to engage meaningfully with discussions around the text and shows an interest in learning more about the topic.

Formal assessment 1

To assess the main learning objectives in Units 1, 2 and 3, have learners do Formal assessment 1 independently. Mark the assessment and record relevant assessment information.

Mark scheme

Question 1

Reading

A (5)

flotsam – driftwood/wreckage/debris

cobbled – joined/sewed

spiritless – dead

floundering – struggling

cloven – stuck

B He has no hope of being rescued. He has no food or water. He is marooned at sea. (2)

C A big, blue tomb. (1)

D 'like a sauna' – this shows how hot it is. The temperature is being compared to the heat of steam in a sauna. (2)

E The sea is flat. (1)

F The man has been shipwrecked. He has no water and is surrounded by sharks that have followed him for three days. (2)

G Alliteration: Dead man drifting, stabbed by a million sun spears. (1)

H Open question. (Could he be going from one 'hell' to another?) (2)

I The shipwrecked sailor's perspective. 'My blood simmers'. (2)

J First person. (1)

K Vocabulary of the sailor: But lo! (1)

Question 2

Grammar

A (4)

Word from text	Part of speech
water	common noun
doomed	adjective
wooden	adjective
emptiness	abstract noun

B (4)
- Adverb of manner
- Proper noun
- Proper adjective
- Adverbial phrase of time

C (4)
- It is important to check your boat before going out to sea.
- The fisherman's adventure was dangerous!
- Have you ever had a lucky escape?
- Always pack extra food, warm clothing and a flare.

D (4)
- The man thought he was safe.
- His ordeal was over.
- I think the sailor was brave.
- The man was on a raft.

E (4)
- Description
- Confidence
- Fragrance
- musician

Unit 4 It's about time

Unit overview

As learners work through this unit, they will explore how authors deal with the concept of time in various texts. They will examine and analyse three different texts, each dealing with time in a different way. 'The Giver' is a science fiction text, dealing with the future, 'Tuck Everlasting' explores how each person's time on Earth must end, and 'What happened to the dinosaurs?' deals with unexplained events from the past. Learners will be guided to note the characteristics of narrative and journalistic-style texts and will be given the opportunity to write their own short science fiction story.

Unit 4	Reading	Writing	Listening and speaking
It's about time Texts *The Giver*, science fiction *Tuck Everlasting*, fiction, extended narrative *What happened to the dinosaurs?* Non-fiction, formal and impersonal	6R01 Articulate personal responses to reading, with close reference to the text. 6R02 Revise different word classes. 6Ri1 Consider how the author manipulates the reaction of the reader, e.g. how characters and settings are presented. 6Ri2 Look for implicit meanings, and make plausible inferences from more than one point in the text. 6Rw1 Comment on a writer's use of language, demonstrating awareness of its impact on the reader. 6Rw2 Explore proverbs, sayings and figurative expressions. 6Rw3 Analyse the success of writing in evoking particular moods, e.g. suspense. 6Rw4 Begin to show awareness of the impact of a writer's choices of sentence length and structure. 6Rw5 Understand the use of conditionals, e.g. to express possibility. 6Rv3 Revise language conventions and	6W01 Continue to learn words, apply patterns and improve accuracy in spelling. 6Wa2 Develop some imaginative detail through careful use of vocabulary and style. 6Wa7 Adapt the conventions of the text type for a particular purpose. 6Wa12 Use different genres as models for writing. 6Wt1 Plan plot, characters and structure effectively in writing an extended story. 6Wt2 Use paragraphs, sequencing and linking them appropriately to support overall development of the text. 6Wt3 Manage the development of an idea throughout a piece of writing, e.g. link the end to the beginning. 6Wt4 Use a range of devices to support cohesion within paragraphs. 6Wp1 Use a wider range of connectives to clarify relationships between ideas, e.g. however, therefore, although.	6SL1 Express and explain ideas clearly, making meaning explicit and respond to guidance about, and feedback on, the quality of contributions. 6SL2 Use spoken language well to persuade, instruct or make a case, e.g. in a debate. 6SL5 Speak confidently in formal and informal contexts. 6SL6 Pay close attention in discussion to what others say, asking and answering questions to introduce new ideas.

	grammatical features of different types of text. 6Rw6 Discuss and express preferences in terms of language, style and themes. 6Rw7 Understand aspects of narrative structure, e.g. the handling of time. 6Rw8 Analyse how paragraphs and chapters are structured and linked. 6Rw13 Identify uses of the semi-colon. 6Rv1 Recognise key characteristics of a range of non-fiction text types. 6Rv2 Understand the conventions of standard English usage in different forms of writing. 6Rv3 Revise language conventions and grammatical features of different types of text. 6Rv8 Begin to develop awareness that the context for which the writer is writing and the context in which the reader is reading can impact on how the text is understood.	6Wp5 Punctuate speech and use apostrophes accurately. 6Ws1 Learn word endings with different spellings but the same pronunciation, -sion, -ssion;	

Related resources
- Audio files: *The Giver*; *Tuck Everlasting*; *What happened to the dinosaurs?*
- PCM 10: Sentences with adjectives
- PCM 11: Sentence work
- PCM 12: Structure of a story
- PCM 13: Spelling

Introducing the unit
Ask learners to describe a perfect school. Guide them to approach the task realistically. When their responses show that they realise that what is perfect for one person may well not be perfect for another, write the following two words on the board: 'utopia' and 'dystopia'. Ask learners to use their dictionaries to find out the meaning of 'utopia' and then to use their knowledge of prefixes to infer the meaning of 'dystopia'. In small groups, ask learners to list the characteristics of a utopian society. Let the groups compare their responses. If you have time, show the similarities and differences of the groups' responses in the form of a Venn diagram.

Week 1

Student's Book pages 40–46

Workbook pages 20–23

Introduction
If possible, play the official film trailer of *The Giver* (http://bit.ly/OwzKMf) in class.

Student's Book pages 40–41
Reading and speaking
1 Read through, and discuss, the definition of science fiction on page 40 of the Student's Book. Let learners discuss the answers to the questions in small groups.

Example answers
a Signs of a perfect world: peace, justice, freedom, choices
b No – let learners explore this concept by sharing their individual opinions
c Let learners share their stories
d Let learners share their opinions

2 Instruct learners to read through the text independently, making note of any strange words they come across.

Student's Book page 42
Comprehension

Example answers
a Science fiction – accept any of the following explanations: the story includes technology of the future, explaining what effect new discoveries, happenings and scientific developments will have on us in the future. Science fiction texts are often set in the future, in space, on a different world, or in a different universe or dimension.
b Compare setting – time and place
c Answers will most likely include discussions of family structure, games etc
d Christening/Baptism
e Newly born baby. This could have been written as one word to 'dehumanise' the baby. There is no sense that this is a miracle of life.
f 'Groupmates' dehumanises the concept of friendship. There is no sense of individual connections. There is an emphasis on groups
g Some learners will say 'no' referring to maturity of age etc. Others may refer to children being forced to take on adult roles due to circumstances beyond their control. (Aids orphans. Genocide etc)
h "But today we honour your differences. They have determined your futures." This statement is ironic as no children were allowed to be different in any way, yet their differences were seen, nonetheless!
i 3rd person omniscient
j To emphasise Jonas' turmoil, his sudden understanding of the strangeness of the situation.

Before continuing with the unit, discuss the features and structure of the extract learners have just examined. As the discussion progresses, write key words on the board. Typical words would be: fiction, science fiction, characters, story, untrue, paragraphs, written for enjoyment. (In the final week of this unit, learners will be asked to compare the three different texts, so this exercise would be a valuable way to focus their attention on the structures of different texts.)

Student's Book page 42
Grammar
Revise the structure of a simple sentence. Stress that a simple sentence does not mean that the sentence is uncomplicated – it means that the sentence contains one idea. Revise that a sentence generally consists of a subject and a predicate. Explain that a simple sentence can even consist of one word, such as 'Run!' In this case, the sentence would only consist of a predicate. Explain that some sentences do not have an obvious subject, such as commands. We say, in these circumstances that the subject of the sentence is 'you understood'. Thus the subject of 'Fetch the water' is 'you understood'. Give learners a selection of sentences, with and without obvious subjects, to analyse verbally.

Let learners complete the activity in their books.

Possible responses to expanding sentences activity:
a The damaged spaceship crashed violently on the barren moon.
b My best friend avidly read a science fiction novel last month.
c The worried astronauts carefully watched the blinking control panel.
d Space travel is terribly expensive.
e Space exploration is extremely dangerous.

Workbook page 20

Grammar

Let learners complete the activity on Workbook page 20.

Some examples of sentences that can be created in the worksheet.
- Brave children paddled in the icy sea currents.
- My brother is a funny British athlete.

Differentiation

Support

Let learners who need extra support complete PCM 10: Sentences with adjectives.

Extension

1 Once learners have written their sentences, let them find synonyms for the descriptive adjectives.

2 Learners can write their own diamante poems

Diamantes are seven lines long.

The first and last lines have just one word.

The second and sixth lines have two words.

The third and fifth lines have three words.

And the fourth line has four words.

Lines 1, 4, and 7 have nouns.

Lines 2 and 6 have adjectives.

Lines 3 and 5 have verbs.

3 Let learners write the sentences in the past tense/future tense.

Student's Book page 43

Punctuation

One of the biggest challenges facing developing writers is showing where their sentences end. This is possibly because they write as they speak, and do not realise that with speech, we can ramble on and still make sense, but that the same is not true when we write.

Write the following on the board:

Let's eat Grandpa.

Ask the class what this sentence means. Then write the following on the board, underneath the first sentence:

Let's eat, Grandpa.

Again ask what the sentence means. Show how the placement of a comma changes the meaning of a sentence. Use this explanation as an introduction to the importance of punctuating the ends of sentences. Link your explanation to the previous grammar exercise on subjects and predicates.

Answers

1
a He wept. He was afraid now that he could not save Gabriel. He no longer cared about himself.
b My instructors in science and technology have taught us about how the brain works. It's full of electrical impulses. It's like a computer.
c He hunched his shoulders. He tried to make himself smaller in the seat.

2
Jonas lives in a world in which there is no pain, no war and very little emotion. In this utopia, everything is as pleasant as possible. Birthmothers give birth to 'newchildren' and never see them again. These 'newchildren' then move to the nurturing centre, and then to a family unit. When they become sick or too old, they are 'released'.
Jonas often sees flashes of change when he looks at an object. He does not realise that he is perceiving colour which disappeared once the community went over to sameness.
At the ceremony, Jonas is chosen to become the new receiver - a respected task that consists of keeping all of the old memories of the community.

Workbook pages 21–22

Punctuation

Answers

The astronauts checked the instruments in the space ship. They were pleased that nothing was wrong.
The astronauts checked the instruments in the space ship; they were pleased that nothing was wrong.
The astronauts checked the instruments in the space ship and they were pleased that nothing was wrong.
Aliens have landed. Have you seen them?
Aliens have landed; have you seen them?
Aliens have landed, but have you seen them?
Dinosaurs once walked on Earth; no-one knows why they died out.
Dinosaurs once walked on Earth. No-one knows why they died out.
Dinosaurs once walked on Earth, yet no-one knows why they died out.
Shooting stars are beautiful to watch. They remind me of fireworks.
Shooting stars are beautiful to watch; they remind me of fireworks.
Shooting stars are beautiful to watch as they remind me of fireworks.

Support

Give learners additional sentences that have been jumbled up and let them rearrange the words sensibly. Use PCM 11: Sentence work.

Answers
1
a Have you read a good book lately?
b There are seven days in a week.
c Time travel must be exciting!
d We all need to be able to make our own decisions.
e A story is a journey of ideas.
f There is no war or pain in Jonas' world.
g Would you choose to live in such a world?
h Newchildren are allocated to family units.
i Jonas was different because he saw flashes of colour.
j Everyone was the same.
2
a Jonas and his friends <u>rode bicycles</u>.
b The children <u>sat on chairs</u>.
c The family units <u>ate their meals at the same time</u>.
d <u>Do</u> you <u>play sport at school?</u>
e <u>Can</u> you <u>choose your own career?</u>
3
a Maria is my cousin.
b My brother and I plan to watch a movie tonight.
c Pizza is my favourite food.
d Madrid is the capital of my country.
e Bears are dangerous animals.

Student's Book page 44

Reading

Thinking deeper

When learners fully understand the impact of conflict in their writing, their story-writing will flourish. It is important that they realise that there can be more than one type of conflict in a story, but that depending on which conflict is seen as the prime focus, so the plot will be influenced. Let learners complete the matching exercise.

Answers
a human vs environment
b human vs self
c human *vs* man
d human vs society
e human vs the unknown
f human *vs* machine/Technology

Instruct learners to work in pairs. Tell them to brainstorm the titles of plays, novels and poems and match these to the different types of conflict. If time allows, discuss this as a class.

Support

1 Find or draw pictures of scenes showing the different types of conflict. Flash the pictures and let learners name the type of conflict.

2 Let learners draw their own interpretations of the types of conflict.

Extension

Divide learners into small groups. Write each type of conflict on a separate piece of paper. Fold the paper so that no writing is visible. Give each group one of the pieces of paper. Instruct the groups to act out short scenes that revolve around the conflict they have been given. Let the rest of the class guess the conflict type.

Student's Book page 45

Reading and writing

If possible, draw the storyline graph on the board. Alternatively, draw your learners' attention to it in Student's Book. The graph visually defines the structure of a short story. Discuss the different sections of a story. It would also be helpful if you were to draw a similar graph but, this time, lengthen the setting. You could also rather shorten the rising action. This will open up understanding of how to manipulate the pace of a plot etc. Make sure that your learners understand, and can name, the structure of a story.

Ask learners to identify the elements of a fairy tale. Write these on the board. Possible suggestions would be:

- Do *not* need to include fairies.
- Include fantasy, supernatural or make-believe characters.
- Clearly defined good characters and evil characters.
- Involves magic elements.
- Often have a conflict or problem that needs to be solved.
- Often have happy endings.
- Usually teach a lesson or demonstrate important values.

Workbook pages 23–24

Reading

1 Let learners complete the exercise.

Answers
1 a pretty young girl is dressed in rags and is scrubbing the floor; **2** an invitation arrives from the palace; **3** the step-sisters and step-mother go to the ball, beautifully dressed; **4** Cinderella is left behind, feeling sad; **5** her fairy godmother arrives; **6** Cinderella goes to the ball wearing a beautiful dress; **7** she dances with the prince; **8** the clock strikes 12 and she runs down the stairs, leaving behind a glass slipper; **9** the prince looks for the owner of the slipper; **10** the step-sisters try on the slipper; **11** Cinderella tries on the slipper and it fits; **12** she marries the prince.

Student's Book pages 45–46
Reading and writing
1 Read the summary outline of Little Red Riding Hood in the table. To reinforce the concept of conflict in literature, discuss the conflict in a well-known fairy tale such as Little Red Riding Hood. In the story, 'Little Red riding Hood' there are different types of conflict to be seen. Discuss how conflict drives the plot of a story.

Conflict type	Conflict in story
Man against man	Red riding hood stops to pick flowers and tells the wolf she is going to visit her grandmother after her mother had told her not to.
Man against self	Red Riding Hood decides whether or not to obey her mother's instructions
Man against the environment	Red Riding Hood's father kills the wolf

2 Put learners into pairs. Give each learner a copy of PCM 12: Structure of a story. Instruct the pairs to choose their own fairy tale and to analyse it according to the table. Guide them to notice that each section of a story could be written as its own paragraph. Thus, if they plan their stories according to the structure table, they will automatically have their paragraphs worked out. Obviously more complex rising and falling actions will need additional paragraphs, but this is a very good starting point.

Student's Book page 46
Writing
1 Learners choose a topic and plan, and then write, their own short story. Remind them about the use of paragraphs.

Differentiation
Support
Divide learners into groups of the same ability. Give each group a story to analyse in the terms of its conflict. Instruct learners to identify and name the conflict in the stories.

Extension
a Divide learners into groups of the same ability. Instruct learners to identify and name the conflict in the stories. Then let the groups change the conflict in whichever way they choose, and explore how the plot changes!
b Encourage learners to read 'The Giver'
c Show the movie 'The Giver' to the class.

Weekly review

Level	Reading	Writing	Listening and speaking
■	Learner has not shown sufficient understanding of the science fiction genre.	Learner has a poor understanding of the structure of a short story. Weak paragraphing makes reading difficult.	Learner does not actively engage in class discussions.
●	A good understanding of the science fiction genre has been shown. Learner has engaged well with the text and has generally answered questions with good insight.	Learner has shown a sound understanding of the structure of a short story. Good use of paragraphs and sentence structure.	Learner contributes to class discussions and is able to generally engage appropriately with peers.
▲	Learner has shown an excellent understanding of the nuances of the science fiction genre.	Learner has written a creative and original short story. Structure is excellent, with good use of conflict.	Learner takes a lead in class discussions. Is able to engage appropriately in discussions.

Week 2

Student's Book pages 47–52

Workbook pages 24–26

Student's Book page 47
Writing and speaking

Discuss the concept of eternal youth with your learners. Ask them what they think the perfect age would be to stop growing older.

Instruct learners to write down ten positive points about living forever as well as ten negative points. Tell them to discuss their ideas in small groups before they listen to an extract from *Tuck Everlasting* by Natalie Babbitt.

If possible, play the recording of the extract, or, alternatively, read it yourself to the class. After you have read the extract to the class, divide learners into pairs and instruct them to discuss what the wheel/circle of life is and how it impacts on our lives. Then, as a class, discuss life cycles, including those occurring in nature.

Student's Book page 49
Comprehension

Answers
a The Tucks have drunk a potion which has caused them to live forever.
b The underlined words in the sentence: 'Winnie, newly brave with her thoughts of being rescued, climbed boldly into the rowboat' shows that Winnie had been frightened before, but was no longer.
c Man against self – does Winnie tell the Tuck's secret?
Man against man – does Winnie run away?
Man against self – does Winnie drink the potion?
Man against the unknown – Does Winnie drink the potion?
d Third Person – omniscient
e Open question. Refer to the Digital slide of the lifecycle of a butterfly
f Time in *The Giver* is set in the future, and is treated realistically. In *Tuck Everlasting* time as an everlasting concept is questioned.
g Positive outcomes: no death, avoid illness and old age etc
h Negative outcomes: over population, financial implications on the economy
i Open question

Extension

Let learners watch a video extract from the film version of *Tuck Everlasting*. Divide them into pairs and let them compare the book extract to the film version.

Workbook pages 24–25
Figurative Language

Answers

Blue	Yellow	Green	Yellow
Green	Blue	Yellow	Blue
Blue	Yellow	Green	Green
Yellow	Red	Yellow	Blue
Yellow	Green	Red	Blue
Green	Blue	Yellow.	Yellow
Blue	Yellow	Green	Yellow
Blue	Yellow	Yellow	Blue

Student's Book pages 49–50
Grammar

Read through the definitions of figurative language. Ask learners to give examples of each type from texts they have read.

Discuss the images created by the following descriptions that have been taken from the extract.

- **The sky was a ragged blaze of red and pink and orange** – The author wants the reader to picture the vibrant sunset filled with vivid colour.
- **… and its double trembled on the surface of the pond like colour spilled from a paint box.** – the reflection of the sunset is seen on the pond.
- **The sun was dropping fast now, a soft red sliding egg yolk** – the sun is round and red, dropping below the horizon
- **The hard heels of her buttoned boots made a hollow banging sound against its wet boards, loud in the warm and breathless quiet** – it is extremely quiet and Winnie's shoes bang against the wooden boards of the boat.
- **Here and there the still surface of the water dimpled, and bright rings spread noiselessly and vanished** – fish are bobbing to the surface, creating rings in the water.

As preparation for reading the third text, discuss the features of the extract from *Tuck Everlasting*. Remind learners of their responses to the first text. Write down learners' responses. Possible responses could be: fiction, paragraphs, characters, fantasy, descriptive writing, figurative language, direct speech.

Support

Let learners write down all the associations they can make with the following shapes:

The triangle looks like a…
The triangle is the…

This will help develop their understanding of similes and metaphors.

Student's Book page 51
Writing

Find a photograph of a nature scene. Let learners brainstorm nouns and adjectives associated with the photograph. Write these on the board. Choose learners at random to create sentences to describe the photograph. Challenge stronger learners to create sentences that include figurative language.

1 Instruct learners to complete the brain storming activity. Record some of the learners' ideas on the board and discuss their merits.

2 Instruct learners to work independently, using the ideas they have brain stormed to write a descriptive paragraph. Revise the structure of a descriptive paragraph.

Student's Book page 51
Spelling

Write the following three verbs on the board: *discussion, conclude* and *supervise*.

Establish with your class that these words are verbs. Ask random learners to use the words in sentences. Then ask how the verbs can be changed into nouns. As soon as a learner responds correctly, write the answer underneath the original verb. Point out that *discussion* has *ssion*, whilst *conclusion* has *sion*. Read the two verbs aloud. Ask the class what they notice about the *sion* sound. Explain that if the word *shin* can be heard, the noun is spelt *ssion*.

Now write on the board: *televise, transfuse, supervise* and *conclude*.

Ask random learners to change the verbs into nouns. Write the correct responses on the board. Ask learners to work out a tip for spelling the nouns correctly. (If the last syllable has a long vowel sound, drop the *e* and add *sion*.)

Read through the spelling rule and let learners complete the spelling activity.

Answers
Discuss – discussion
Confess – confession
Regress – regression
Obsess – obsession
Impress – impression

Collide – collision
Corrode – corrosion
Invade – invasion
Conclude – conclusion

Transfuse – transfusion
Confuse – confusion
Televise – television
Supervise – supervision

Differentiation
Support

Let learners complete PCM 13: Spelling

Extension

If you have access to the internet, let learners log on to the spellzone website. Click on one of the spelling rule options on the right hand side of the page which will take you to spelling games. This is a free site, but limited to certain activities.

Student's Book page 52
Grammar

1 Read through the rules for direct speech.

2 Let learners complete the activity in their books.

Example answer
a Winnie asked, "Why does life have to be so complicated?"
"Why does life have to be so complicated?," asked Winnie.
"Why," asked Winnie, "does life have to be so complicated?"
b Tuck replied, "It's not complicated, Winnie. Life is very simple. It follows a natural path."
"It's not complicated, Winnie. Life is very simple. It follows a natural path," replied Tuck.
"It's not complicated," replied Tuck. "Life is very simple. It follows a natural path."
c Winnie exclaimed, "But I would love to live forever!"
"But I would love to live forever!" exclaimed Winnie.
"But," exclaimed Winnie, "I would love to live forever!"
d Tuck asked," Would that be natural, Winnie?"
"Would that be natural Winnie?" asked Tuck.
"Would that," asked Tuck, "be natural Winnie?"

Workbook page 26

Grammar

Answers

Spog asked, "Why don't aliens eat clowns?"
Sperkle replied, "Because they taste funny!"
Spog asked, "What did Mars say to Saturn?"
Sperkle replied. "Give me a ring sometime!"
"How do you organise a space party?" asked Spog.
"You planet!" laughed Sperkle.
Spog asked, "How do you get a baby astronaut to sleep?"
Sperkle answered, "You rocket!"

Weekly review

Level	Reading	Grammar	Listening and speaking
■	Learner has not engaged with the text or been able to follow written instructions accurately. Learner struggles to interpret figurative language.	Learner has little understanding of direct speech. Very basic vocabulary used in descriptive paragraph.	Learner shows little interest in class discussions.
●	Learner is able to identify figurative language fairly consistently and is making progress in understanding the nuances of such descriptions.	Learner is developing an understanding of direct speech. Fairly good vocabulary used in descriptive paragraph.	Learner engages positively in discussions.
▲	Learner has engaged fully with the text and intuitively appreciates the nuances of figurative language.	Accurate punctuation of direct speech. Excellent imagery created in descriptive paragraph.	Learner shows great interest in the topic and the opinions of others.

Week 3

Student's Book pages 52–54

Student's Book page 52

Speaking

Source a photograph of a dinosaur and project this on a screen. Hold a general discussion on prehistoric creatures. Continue the discussion using the illustrations on Student's Book page 52.

Before they read the extract, instruct learners to take note of its format.

Student's Book page 54

Speaking

Example answers
a The aim of the text is to give factual information about the existence of dinosaurs and to explore theories why the disappeared. The text has been written to provide information about dinosaurs. It is non-fiction.
b The text was most likely written for children in middle school. We can assume this by examining the type of vocabulary being used.
c The writing style of 'What happened to the Dinosaurs' is factual and informative. It is non-fiction. Tuck Everlasting is a narrative that is filled with figurative language. 'The Giver' is also a narrative, but is a science fiction story.
d Open question.

Hold a class discussion about the functions and structures of different texts. For example: dictionaries, encyclopaedias, recipes, instruction pamphlets, songs, shopping lists, text messages.

Student's Book page 54
Comprehension

By now learners should be able to work independently to find the answers using the text as they need to.

a Open question.
b About 65 million years ago they simply seemed to disappear.
c Pangaea is called a supercontinent because about 250 million years ago all the continents were joined together.
d We know that dinosaurs existed because scientists have found dinosaur fossils in rocks around the world.
e The ash from the volcanoes could possibly have caused the climate to change. Open question.
f Open question – learner must show an understanding of the question.
g The answer lies buried under the ground in the ancient rocks of the fossil recorded. We'll need to find out a lot more about fossils before we discover the truth about the disappearing dinosaurs.

Weekly review

Level	Reading	Listening and speaking
■	Learner is not able to examine the text closely for details. Learner still has little understanding of text types.	Learner contributes very little to class discussions and does not express opinions.
●	Learner is able to accurately answer most questions based on the text. Learner has a fairly good understanding of text types.	Learner engages well with texts and is able to articulate opinions.
▲	Learner shows full understanding of the text. Learner shows a thorough understanding of text types.	Learner engages fully with all kinds of texts and is able to accurately articulate viewpoints and opinions.

Unit 5 Facts, foibles and fables

Unit overview

In this unit, learners will be given the opportunity to explore the same topic from both a fiction and non-fiction perspective. They will be challenged to evaluate their own pre-conceived ideas and will also be expected to be able to justify and explain their opinions. 'Creepy Crawlies' is a non-fiction text that learners will find interesting as it illustrates creatures that many people are afraid of. To balance this, learners will then work through a more philosophical text, a myth exploring the reasons for evils being in the world. Finally, learners will engage with a poem on mosquitoes, but again, their pre-conceived ideas will be challenged, as the poet is actually sympathetic towards these insects.

There are opportunities for learners to continue developing their writing skills, and they will be continually guided to revise word classes and learn the techniques for structuring sentences.

Unit 5	Reading	Writing	Listening and speaking
Facts, foibles and fables *Phobias*, non-fiction formal and impersonal Blurb and extracts from *Weird Monsters*, non-fiction, formal and impersonal *The Fox and the Crow*, fiction, fable *Holes*, fiction, story with flashbacks *Mosquitoes*, poem	6R01 Articulate personal responses to reading, with close reference to the text. 6R02 Revise different word classes. 6R03 Develop familiarity with the work of established authors and poets, identifying features which are common to more than one text. 6Rx1 Distinguish between fact and opinion in a range of texts and other media. 6Rx2 Paraphrase explicit meanings based on information from more than one point in the text. 6Ri1 Consider how the author manipulates the reaction of the reader, e.g. how characters and settings are presented. 6Ri2 Look for implicit meanings, and make plausible inferences from more than one point in the text. 6Rw1 Comment on a writer's use of language, demonstrating awareness of its impact on the reader.	6W01 Continue to learn words, apply patterns and improve accuracy in spelling. 6Wa1 Establish and maintain a clear viewpoint, with some elaboration of personal voice. 6Wa7 Adapt the conventions of the text type for a particular purpose. 6Wa8 Select appropriate non-fiction style and form to suit specific purposes. 6Wa9 Write non-chronological reports linked to work in other subjects. 6Wa12 Use different genres as models for writing. 6Wt1 Plan plot, characters and structure effectively in writing an extended story. 6Wt2 Use paragraphs, sequencing and linking them appropriately to support overall development of the text. 6Wt4 Use a range of devices to support cohesion within	6SL1 Express and explain ideas clearly, making meaning explicit and respond to guidance about, and feedback on, the quality of contributions. 6SL5 Speak confidently in formal and informal contexts. 6SL6 Pay close attention in discussion to what others say, asking and answering questions to introduce new ideas. 6SL7 Help to move group discussion forward, e.g. by clarifying, summarising. 6SL8 Prepare, practise and improve a spoken presentation or performance. 6SL9 Convey ideas about characters in drama in different roles and scenarios through deliberate choice of speech, gesture and movement.

| | 6Rw2 Explore proverbs, sayings and figurative language. 6Rw4 Begin to show awareness of the impact of a writer's choices of sentence length and structure. 6Rw5 Understand the use of conditionals, e.g. to express possibility. 6Rw8 Analyse how paragraphs and chapters are structured and linked. 6Rw9 Read and interpret poems in which meanings are implied or multilayered. 6Rw10 Explore how poets manipulate and play with words and their sounds. 6Rv1 Recognise key characteristics of a range of non-fiction text types. 6Rv3 Revise language conventions and grammatical features of different types of text. 6Rv4 Compare the language, style and impact of a range of non-fiction writing. 6Rv8 Begin to develop awareness that the context for which the writer is writing and the context in which the reader is reading can impact on how the text is understood. | paragraphs. 6Wt5 Use connectives to structure an argument or discussion. 6Wp1 Use a wider range of connectives to clarify relationships between ideas, e.g. *however, therefore, although*. 6Wp2 Develop grammatical control of complex sentences, manipulating them for effect. 6Wp3 Distinguish the main clause and other clauses in a complex sentence. 6Wp4 Develop increasing accuracy in using punctuation effectively to mark out the meaning in complex sentences. 6Ws2 Use correct choices when representing consonants, e.g. 'ck'/'k'/'ke'/'que'/'ch'; 6Ws3 Further investigate spelling rules and exceptions, including representing unstressed vowels. 6Ws6 Explore word origins and derivations and the use of words from other languages. 6Ws7 Investigate meanings and spellings of connectives. | |

Related resources

- Audio files: *Phobias*; *World's Deadliest Creatures*; *The Fox and the Crow*; *Mosquitoes*
- PCM 14: Summary table
- PCM 15: The structure of a sentence
- PCM 16: More about sentences

Weeks 1 and 2

Student's Book pages 55–61

Workbook pages 27–29

Introducing the unit

It is quite possible that this section of the unit will take longer than a week, so we've combined Week 1 and 2. The grammar, in particular, may be quite challenging.

Disply the word *Arachibutyrophobia*. Ask learners what they think it means and let them explain their reasooning. Explain the *phobia* is a suffix meaning 'an extreme or irrational fear of something'. Discuss the distinction between a rational fear and one that is irrational. This phobia is the fear of peanut butter sticking to the roof of the mouth!

Show the class some photographs of everyday items and have them make up sensible words to describe an irrational fear of that item.

Student's Book pages 55–56

Reading and speaking

1 Read the information.

2 Place learners into small groups and let them discuss the opening questions.

3 The correct definition of glossophobia is 'fear of public speaking'. Discuss the learners' experiences of this condition.

4 Place learners in pairs and instruct them to think of a scenario that could lead to the fear of peanut butter sticking to the roof of one's mouth. Walk around the class during the paired discussion, and choose the most interesting/creative scenarios to be shared with the rest of learners.

5 Instruct the groups to choose a phobia from the list, to research its meaning, and to create a short scene to explain how their phobia came into existence. If time allows, let all the groups showcase their work, otherwise, just choose the most original and well-prepared acts. Comment on the strengths of each performance.

Leukophobia: Fear of the colour white
Xanthophobia: Fear of the colour yellow
Nephophobia: Fear of clouds
Melanophobia: Fear of the colour black
Ereuthophobia: Fear of the colour red
Arithmophobia: Fear of numbers
Peladophobia: Fear of bald people
Trichopathophobia: Fear of the number 13

Student's Book pages 57–58

Reading

1 Have a few books on hand, and show learners what a 'blurb' is. You may even read a few out to the class. Read through the blurb on page 57 of the Student's Book. Briefly discuss the two questions that follow the blurb.

2 Instruct learners to read the text carefully. Draw learners' attention to the layout of the text that follows. Direct specific questions to random learners about the use of headings, pictures etc.

Workbook pages 27–28

Comprehension

Completing this activity in small groups will prepare learners for the final comprehension question. Alternatively, it could be done as a reinforcement exercise after learners have completed the comprehension activity.

Answers
1 Katydid 2 Mudskipper 3 Cicada
4 Leaf chameleon 5 Praying Mantis, Leaf-tailed gecko, Leaf chameleon, Mossy frog,
6 Saddleback caterpillar 7 Venus Flytrap – it's a plant and all others are animals

Student's Book page 58

Comprehension

Let learners discuss the answers to the questions in pairs before writing the answers in their books independently. To save time, you could give each learner a copy of PCM 14: Summary table to complete for question 10.

Example answers
a Open question.
b Open question.
c It would not be acceptable as the measurement is not scientifically based and has too many variables such as the size of people's hands.
d In the text, there is a drawing of a creature next to a hand to show the scale.
e It would not be a good idea as spiders are not insects, nor are scorpions or mossy frogs. A title has to be accurate in a non-fiction text, else the text will not be trustworthy. (Refer to this site for further discussion: http://www.explorit.org/science/spider.html)
f Although the text is non-fiction, it has not been written formally. It is more conversational in style. (Compare this style to a Wikipedia extract)
g The writer has written in a conversational style so that the content will be more accessible to younger readers.

h The style would not be appropriate for a lecture as it is too informal and too similar to a narrative.

i Children doing research on strange creatures. The text is easy to understand and is logically presented.

j

Creepy Crawly	Habitat	Eating habits	Appearance	Hunting method	Interesting Facts
Praying Mantis	Rainforest in Central America	Beetles, moths Eats prey alive	Looks like a leaf Large front legs Spikes on legs	Stays very still. Scoops prey in large front legs. Eats prey alive	Eats prey alive
Tarantula	Burrows in the ground	Crickets, frogs, lizards, cockroaches, mice	hairy	Hunts at night Pounces on prey, injects poisonous venom	Goliath tarantula eats birds. Large as a dinner plate
Scorpion	Hot countries all over the world	Insects, lizards	Small eyes, can't see well Use special hairs on legs to feel their way	Grab small prey with pincers and tear apart. Stings larger prey first.	A meal can last a year
Weta	New Zealand Hide under logs or in holes	Leaves, seeds, small insects	One of world's largest insects Up to 90mm long, heavy as a bird		Existed 200 million years ago Can survive underwater for 4 days. Some survive after being frozen solid.
Mossy Frog	Near streams and rivers in Vietnam, south-east Asia	Hunts at night Small insects	Bumpy green and brown skin Large eyes Suckers on each toe	Pounces on prey	Pounces on prey

Extension
- Let learners research different phobias
- Let learners set their own questions based on the tabulated information. They could work in pairs for this exercise.

Student's Book pages 59–60

Grammar
Before you begin the next section on grammar, revise adverbs, adjectives and sentence structure. Remind learners that every sentence must contain a verb. Give each learner a copy of PCM 15: The structure of a sentence as a reinforcement activity.

Answers to PCM 15
1
a The wind was howling and I was freezing.
b It was raining, but it didn't matter!
c The bird flew away for it got a fright.
d I may watch TV or I may play outside.
(There is no comma if only two items are listed.)
e It's sunny outside, so I'm going to swim.
2 a l b C c C d l e l f C g l

Write a selection of simple sentences on flashcards. Divide learners into small groups and give each group a flashcard. Instruct the groups to 'drop in' some extra information. (Learners may not know the metalanguage for what they are doing, but they will instinctively add in adjectives, adverbs, a phrase or a clause.) Let the groups read their original sentence aloud, and then their new sentence.

Before you read through the notes on complex sentences, it would be simplest to first consolidate learners' understanding of compound sentences. Once they understand that there are a limited number of co-ordinate conjunctions, (FANBOYS), it will be easy to identify the subordinate conjunctions by default. Read through the notes on connectives.

Answers

1
a The mantis looks like a leaf <u>so</u> that other insects don't notice it.(CC)
b The mossy frog has special suckers on each toe to help it cling to rocks <u>and</u> branches.(CC)
c A tarantula rears up and shows its enormous fangs to scare enemies.(CC)
d Never pick up a scorpion <u>because</u> their stings can make you very ill. (SC)
e Wetas have probably survived for such a long time <u>as</u> they are tough. (SC)
2 Open question.
3 Example answers
a Because they live for over 30 years, Tarantulas are called spider superstars.
b In order to scare its enemies, Tarantulas rear up and show their fangs.
c Because there where wetas on Earth during the time of the dinosaurs, they are often called insect dinosaurs.
d As they are tough, Wetas have survived for so long.
e Because their poisonous stingers can make you very ill, scorpions should never be picked up.
4 Example answers:
a If I had to see a spider on my arm, I would scream!
b If I could choose a pet, I would pick a kitten.
c If it rains tomorrow, we'll have to stay indoors.
d If you oversleep, you'll miss the bus.

Workbook page 29

Grammar

Example answers
1
a Chirag wouldn't walk through the forest because he was scared of all the spiders!
b I couldn't see the specimen clearly so I took out my microscope.
c I picked up the tarantula even though it was hairy and scary!
- if it's all clear – adverbial clause
- that looks like a frog – adjectival clause
- that look like little arms – adjectival clause, to push itself forward – adverbial clause

d   The spider may bite you if you pick it up.

2
The praying mantis stays very still **so that** it doesn't get noticed by other insects.
The leaf-tailed gecko wakes up at night **and** goes hunting.
The mossy frog will jump into a river **if** there's any danger.
Tarantulas eat cockroaches **and** even mice!
Some Wetas are 90mm long **and** as heavy as a bird.

3

Scorpions are closely related to spiders, mites and ticks	S
Scorpions typically eat insects	S
Hundreds of millions of years	P
In the desert.	P
Scorpions are fluorescent under ultraviolet light.	S
Another key to their survival in so many harsh environments.	P
They are burrowing animals.	S

1

The Venus flytrap is called a plant with an appetite <u>as it eats insects</u>.	Subordinate clause
<u>If a bee or a fly crawls on its leaf</u>, the leaf snaps shut in one-tenth of a second.	Subordinate clause
<u>The leaf oozes chemicals</u> which turn the insects' insides to soup.	Independent clause
<u>After a week or so, the leaf opens again</u> because the plant needs food again.	Independent clause Subordinate clause
These plants eat insects <u>because they live in swamps where it's hard for them to get all the food they need from the soil</u>.	Subordinate clause

Support

PCM 16: More about sentences can be used as an additional activity to support learners who find this difficult.

Student's Book page 61

Writing

Revise the characteristics of a report by skimming through the text again. Discuss the value of headings, pictures etc. make sure that learners use the checklist to make sure they have covered all the bases.

Give your learners the following guidelines:

Choose a topic that interests you

Find information about your topic from two sources.

First draft

Answer these questions:

Where does your creature live?

- Write about five sentences about the habitat.
- Draw a map or find a picture of the habitat.

What does your creature look like?

- Describe its features(colour, size)
- Draw or find a picture of the creature

Why is this a creepy crawly?

How does this creature survive?

Why did you choose this creature?

List all the new words you have learnt with their meanings

Write a topic sentence for each of these headings:

| Habitat | Eating habits | Appearance | Hunting method | Interesting Facts |

Write about five supporting sentences for each topic sentence.

Second draft (Final draft)

Write a title

Write each topic and supporting sentences as a different paragraph. Give the paragraphs headings.

Include any diagrams or photos. Label the diagrams and photos.

Make sure the report is written in the present tense and in the third person.

Write a conclusion. Say why you chose the creature.

Write down the information for a glossary.

Support

Let your weaker learners work in a small group. Provide them with resources (encyclopaedias, websites).

Weekly review

Level	Reading	Writing	Grammar
■	Learner has shown little understanding of the text. Insufficient content has been extrapolated into the table.	Learner has not researched the topic sufficiently. Notes have been poorly structured.	Learner has very poor grasp of complex sentences.
●	Learner has shown a good understanding of the text. A pleasing attempt has been made to summarise and tabulate content.	Learner has put effort into the research of the topic. Notes have been well-written.	Learner has a good grasp of how to create and identify complex sentences.
▲	Learner is able to summarise and tabulate information from a non-fiction text. Learner clearly understands how emotions can cloud perception of texts.	Learner has researched, and written, an excellent report. Interesting and relevant content.	Learner is accurately able to manipulate phrases and clauses in complex sentences.

Weeks 1 and 2 (continued)

Student's Book pages 61–64

Student's Book pages 61–62

Listening and speaking

Revise the characteristics of a fable and compare these to a legend, myth and a fairy tale. Myths, legends and fables are old stories written for adults and children. Folk or fairy tales were written specially for children. Myths are made up stories that try to explain how our world works and how we should treat each other. The stories are usually set in times long ago, before history as we know it was written. Legends are about people and their actions or deeds. The people lived in more recent times and are mentioned in history. The stories are told for a purpose and are based on facts, but they are not completely true. A fable is told to teach a lesson about something and are about animals that can talk and act like people, or plants or forces of nature like thunder or wind. Folk and fairy tales are stories written specially for children, often about magical characters such as elves, fairies, goblins and giants. Sometimes the characters are animals.

1 If possible, play a recording of the fable of *The Fox and the Crow*. Alternatively, read the fable to your class. Instruct learners to discuss the questions following the text, in pairs.

2 Example answers
a Characters are identified by their animal forms.
b Having no specific names gives the story a more universal appeal.
c Open question.

Student's Book page 62

Writing

Instruct learners to write their own fable, using the check list to guide them. (It helps enormously if the conflict is sorted out first.)

Extension
Divide learners into groups. Give each group a different Aesop's Fable to read and dramatise.

Student's Book pages 63–64

Grammar

1 Either play the recording or read the extract from *Holes* by Louis Sachar. Then discuss the different sentence lengths in the extract. Talk about 'artistic licence' allowing an author to write a single word as a sentence. Discuss the impact the one word sentence has on the reader.

2 Instruct learners to copy this table into their books, and to complete it by analysing the extract from *Holes*.

Technique used by the author to create mood	Quote from extract
a Short sentences	Usually. Always.
b Repetition of ideas in a sentence	If you don't **bother** them, they won't **bother** you.
c Starting a sentence with a verb	Being bitten by a scorpion or even a rattlesnake…
d Starting sentences with an adverb	Out on the lake, rattlesnakes and scorpions…
e Starting a sentence with a connector	If you get bitten by a yellow-spotted lizard…
f Speaking directly to the reader	But you don't want to be bitten by…

Weekly review

Level	Reading	Writing	Grammar	Listening and speaking
■	Learner has not been able to identify the 'lessons' behind fables. Learner finds it difficult to interpret nuances of texts.	Learner has not really shown an understanding of the characteristics of a fable.	Learner has little grasp of how authors manipulate mood and the reader through sentence structure.	Learner finds it difficult to participate meaningfully in class discussions.
●	Learner is able to interpret and analyse fables. Learner shows a good understanding of this genre of text.	Learner has written a pleasing fable. It has all the characteristics pertinent to this genre of text.	Learner is beginning to grasp the impact of sentence structure on mood and the reader.	Learner was able to contribute to the class discussions.
▲	Learner has an excellent understanding of the nuances of fables.	Learner has written an entertaining and highly original fable. Excellent use of figurative language.	Learner has a thorough understanding of how to manipulate the reader through the use of varied sentences.	Learner's contributions to class discussions were meaningful and insightful.

Week 3

Student's Book pages 64–66

Workbook page 31

Student's Book page 64

Reading

Read the facts about mosquitoes and have a general conversation about the insect. It is important that learners make definite statements about their opinions of this insect before they read/hear the poem. (The poet embraces mosquitoes, which is an unexpected take on preconceived perceptions of this insect.)

Before learners read the poem, (you may decide to read the poem to them, or play the digital recording), make sure learners know how to identify and interpret similes and metaphors.

Student's Book page 65

Speaking

Place learners in small groups. As this is quite a challenging poem, either group the weaker learners together so that you can work closely with them, or ensure that there is at least one strong learner in every group who could take the lead in the discussion. Remind learners to keep their answers in context of the text.

Example answers
1
a False. They doze on the white ceiling
b True
c False. 'They wish us no harm'
d False. 'Stealing through windows'
e True
f True
g False. Our babies/our own flesh and blood
2
a 'they work like surgeons' 'hanging like fruit bats'
b The mosquito's bite is like a surgeon operating on a human'
c 'the mosquitoes look like fruit bats hanging from the roof of a cave
d 'The mosquitoes are surgeons…'
The mosquitoes are bats…
e They work like seamstresses
Hanging like ripe figs/grapes
3
a Extinct cloaked vampires
b mosquitoes and vampires – both suck human's blood
c Own explanations
d Mosquitoes are like vampires
4 He has described them as blood relations of humans – children
5 They are helpless without us
6 Open question
7 Open question
8 No
9 Open question
10 Open question
11 Open question

Workbook page 31

Spelling and vocabulary

Refer learners back to the statement that Mosquito is Spanish for "little fly" and that in southern Africa, mosquitoes are called "mozzies". Discuss how foreign words have crept into the English language.

Example answers

1

The word we use every day	Meaning	Country
Alligator	The lizard	Spain
Faux pas	A mistake	France
Kaput	Something is broken and useless	Germany
tornado	To turn	Spain
Mammoth	Huge	Russian
cafeteria	Coffee store	Spain
Bandana	Large coloured scarf	Hindi
Déjà vu	Feeling you've experienced something before	France
Gung-ho	Enthusiastic, especially in warfare	China
Bonanza	A source of good fortune and wealth.	Spain
Algebra	Mending broken parts	Arabic
patio	Courtyard	Spain
Tycoon	Great lord	Japan
Ombudsman	Legal representative	Finland
Shawl	Fabric draped around the shoulders	Persia

Student's Book page 66

Spelling

1 Discuss the spelling rule.

2 Let learners read the words aloud.

Support

Let learners play a spelling game online to reinforce this spelling rule.

Student's Book page 66

Writing

Refer learners to the research they had previously completed on a creature of their own choice. Revise the structure of narrative as well as 'point of view'. Instruct learners to use their research to write a narrative paragraph, but this time, from the perspective of the creature itself.

Discuss the question prompts that could help learners plan their ideas. Insist that learners plan their paragraph thoroughly before submitting a final draft.

Extension

Let learners write their paragraph and then turn it into a digital presentation with images, sound effects and music.

Let learner write their own free verse poem about a mosquito.

Weekly review

Level	Reading	Writing	Listening and speaking
■	Learner has not interpreted the poem well. Poor understanding of figurative language is hindering progress. Learner has struggled to interpret the poet's 'voice'. Poor research skills to find the origins of 'borrowed words'.	Learner has struggled to write an interesting narrative. Poor use of perspective.	Learner does not actively participate in group discussions.
●	Learner has shown a good understanding of the poem. Good interpretation of figurative language has aided interpretation. Learner has shown a satisfactory understanding of the spelling rule and has made the effort to find the origins of 'borrowed words'.	Learner has written sufficient content and has made the effort to be original.	Learner generally participates well in group discussions. An effort has been made to make valuable contributions to the topic.
▲	Learner has fully grasped the meaning of the poem, and is able to understand the poet's 'dilemma' of being drawn towards the mosquito. Learner has mastered the spelling rule and is able to apply it consistently. Excellent research of the origins of 'borrowed words'.	Learner has written a delightful and engaging text, with interesting figurative language and a variety of sentence lengths.	Learner engages actively in group discussions, listening to, and responding sensibly to the comments of fellow members.

Unit 6 Holey-moley

Unit overview

This unit focuses on concepts and dimensions of time and space, but not in science-fiction settings. This makes for an interesting discussion at the end of the unit. This unit begins with a non-fiction text about Black Holes – a topic that fascinates even the most reluctant learners. Learners are guided to discuss factual information by answering comprehension questions.

The second text in this unit is an extract from 'Holes'. Learners will be developing their skills to infer information from clues in the text as well be introduced to the 'flashback' technique in literature.

The third text is the poem, 'High Flight' that ties up the concept of space and time.

Learners continue to consolidate connectives and deal with –tch spelling words and prefixes meaning 'not'.

Modern learners must be able to collaborate effectively and efficiently, and this vital skill is developed in this unit's speaking activity.

As writing tasks, learners will create dialogues, write notes for an oral presentation and write their own Kennings poem.

Unit 6	Reading	Writing	Listening and speaking
Holey-moley Texts *Black holes*, non-fiction, formal and impersonal *How to do a presentation*, non-fiction instructions *Holes*, fiction, extended narrative with flashbacks *How to do an oral report as a team*, non-fiction, instructions *High flight*, poem with imagery *My sister*, poem	6R01 Articulate personal responses to reading, with close reference to the text. 6R02 Revise different word classes. 6R03 Develop familiarity with the work of established authors and poets, identifying features which are common to more than one text. 6Rx1 Distinguish between fact and opinion in a range of texts and other media. 6Rx2 Paraphrase explicit meanings based on information from more than one point in the text. 6Ri1 Consider how the author manipulates the reaction of the reader, e.g. how characters and settings are presented. 6Ri2 Look for implicit meanings, and make plausible inferences from more than one point in the text. 6Rw1 Comment on a writer's use of language, demonstrating awareness of its impact on the reader.	6W01 Continue to learn words, apply patterns and improve accuracy in spelling. 6W02 Use handwriting and IT effectively, making appropriate choices of presentation, to prepare writing for publication. 6Wa1 Establish and maintain a clear viewpoint, with some elaboration of personal voice. 6Wa7 Adapt the conventions of the text type for a particular purpose. 6Wa12 Use different genres as models for writing. 6Wt2 Use paragraphs, sequencing and linking them appropriately to support overall development of the text. 6Wt4 Use a range of devices to support cohesion within paragraphs.	6SL1 Express and explain ideas clearly, making meaning explicit and respond to guidance about, and feedback on, the quality of contributions. 6SL2 Use spoken language well to persuade, instruct or make a case, e.g. in a debate. 6SL3 Vary vocabulary, expression and tone of voice to engage the listener and suit the audience, purpose and context. 6SL4 Structure talk to aid a listener's understanding and engagement. 6SL5 Speak confidently in formal and informal contexts. 6SL6 Pay close attention in discussion to what others say, asking and answering questions to introduce new ideas. 6SL7 Help to move group discussion

	6Rw2 Explore proverbs, sayings and figurative expressions.	6Wt5 Use connectives to structure an argument or discussion.	forward, e.g. by clarifying, summarising.
	6Rw3 Analyse the success of writing in evoking particular moods, e.g. suspense.	6Wp1 Use a wider range of connectives to clarify relationships between ideas, e.g. *however, therefore, although*.	6SL8 Prepare, practise and improve a spoken presentation or performance.
	6Rw4 Begin to show awareness of the impact of a writer's choices of sentence length and structure.	6Ws2 Use correct choices when representing consonants, e.g. 'ck'/'k'/'ke'/'que'/'ch'; 'ch'/'tch'; 'j'/'dj'/'dje'.	6SL9 Convey ideas about characters in drama in different roles and scenarios through deliberate choice of speech, gesture and movement.
	6Rw7 Understand aspects of narrative structure, e.g. the handling of time.		
	6Rw8 Analyse how paragraphs and chapters are structured and linked.	6Ws4 Develop knowledge of word roots, prefixes and suffixes, including recognising variations, e.g. im, in, ir, il; ad, ap, af, al and knowing when to use double consonants.	
	6Rw9 Read and interpret poems in which meanings are implied or multilayered.		
	6Rw10 Explore how poets manipulate and play with words and their sounds.		
	6Rv1 Recognise key characteristics of a range of non-fiction text types.	6Ws5 Know how to transform meaning with prefixes and suffixes.	
	6Rv2 Understand the conventions of standard English usage in different forms of writing.	6Ws7 Investigate meanings and spellings of connectives.	
	6Rv3 Revise language conventions and grammatical features of different types of text.		
	6Rv6 Identify features of balance written arguments.		
	6Rv7 Take account of viewpoint in a novel, and distinguish voice of author from that of narrator.		
	6Rv8 Begin to develop awareness that the context for which the writer is writing and the context in which the reader is reading can impact on how the text is understood.		

Related resources
- Audio files: *Dark stars*; *Holes Chapter 1*; *Holes Chapter 2*; *Holes Chapter 3*; *Holes Chapter 6*; *High Flight*; *My Sister*
- PCM 17: Group evaluation
- PCM 18: Connectives

Week 1

Student's Book pages 67–70

Workbook page 32

Introduction to the unit
Introduce the unit by asking learners if any of them would ever want to travel to another planet. Then ask learners if they have heard about the Mars One mission.

Share some of the background information below, or let learners do their own research if they are interested in the topic. Discuss the obstacles the astronauts would face on their adventure as well as the dangers in outer space they would possibly come across. Hopefully one of your learners will mention black holes. If not, introduce this as one of the dangers.

Background information on the Mars One mission

> Julia Harris (staff@latinpost.com) recently reported on the Mars One mission, and wrote that 'a Dutch non-profit organisation, has announced the names of 100 people who will remain in the running for a one-way trip to establish human life on Mars in 2024. There are 50 men and 50 women who successfully passed the second round. The candidates come from all around the world, namely 39 from the Americas, 31 from Europe, 16 from Asia, 7 from Africa, and 7 from Oceania.
>
> More than 200,000 people applied for the chance to live out their lives on Mars. While the plan may sound far-fetched, in December 2013, Colorado-based aerospace giant Lockheed Martin Space Systems agreed to partner with the nonprofit to develop an unmanned spacecraft to land on Mars.
>
> The private project to establish a permanent human colony on Mars is led by 37-year-old Dutch entrepreneur, vBas Lansdorp, who announced the Mars One mission in May 2012. His goal, it seems, is to beat The National Aeronautics and Space Administration (NASA) and the space programs of other counties in landing the first human on Mars.
>
> According to the Washington Post, NASA has no plans to attempt a human-astronaut landing on Mars until the 2030s.
>
> "The astronauts on the International Space Station switch out every couple of months and go back home to family," Norbert Kraft, Mars One's chief medical officer, said in a January interview. "In our case, the astronauts will live together in a group for the rest of their lives."
>
> Kraft interviewed 660 candidates who said they were prepared to leave everything on Earth to live on Mars. The applications were open to anyone over age 18.
>
> Mars One will be televising the competition as it narrows the group down to 24. The remaining 24 people will be divided into six teams of four that will compete to be the most prepared group to leave for Mars in 2024.
>
> Mars One released a trailer for the televised competition, but no air date has been announced.
>
> The cost to send the initial four people to Mars is estimated at $6 billion.

Student's Book page 67

Listening and speaking
Tell learners that they will be evaluating the advantages of group work as one of the skills explored in this unit. Write the following quote from Michael Jordan on the board, or find another, similar, one:

"Talent wins games, but teamwork and intelligence win championships."

Ask a random learner to explain how this applies to school work.

Instruct learners to discuss the introductory questions in groups. Take some time to discuss their answers as class.

Student's Book page 67
Writing

Refer to the picture of the book cover. Use this as an introduction to a discussion on black holes. Instruct learners to take short notes during their group discussion. Remind them that these notes should be short and to the point, most likely consisting only of bullet points and key words.

Workbook page 32
Reading and writing

Let learners complete this activity. This will reinforce their understanding of the difference between facts and opinions.

Student's Book pages 68–69
Reading and speaking

Instruct learners to read the extract. Tell them that they will discuss the facts they have read as a group afterwards. (This would be a good opportunity to let stronger readers read aloud, or each learner could have a turn to read. Alternatively, group the readers according to their reading abilities, and spend more time with the weakest group where you could model the reading.)

Student's Book page 70
Comprehension

Example answers
a Open question.
b The 20th century
c Objects that come close to a black hole get pulled towards it, then disappear into it. Black holes can swallow whole moons, planets and stars.
d A black hole is a tiny invisible point in space.
e If a spaceship flew too close to a black hole, it would get pulled into it.
f When a giant star starts to die, it expands and bursts in a massive explosion called a supernova before shrinking again.
g No. This process can take place over millions of years. First, the star swells up and turns red. Then they shrink and cool down into a small, heavy ball of ash.
h Gravity
i The gravity in a black hole is so strong it changes the shape of objects and compresses them so tightly that they shrink down to nothing.

Student's Book page 70
Writing

You could spend some time talking apps that learners already use on tablets or smartphones. Let them explain how they got the apps onto their devices. Then, let them sequence the given instructions, focussing on the connectives which show the sequence of events.

Answers
- First download the "Show Me" App (search in iTunes)
- Then open the "Show Me" app on your device.
- Next, click 'Create Show Me'. This opens a screen with several tools at the top: draw, write, erase.
- Before you begin recording, add a photo or image as a background in your explanations.
- Click the red record button at the centre top of the screen to record your actions and voice.
- Finally, share with your friends!

Student's Book page 71
Speaking and presenting

Instruct learners to create a digital presentation on black holes. There are many applications which are both free and easy to use. Here is a list of suggested applications:

Microsoft Power point

Haiku Deck

Show Me

Educreations

ScreenChomp

iMovie

Keynote

Presentation skills will be dealt with more formally and extensively later in this unit. It would be extremely helpful if learners reflected on the difficulties they experienced in this activity. Let them write down their reflections. They would then have a reference point later on in the unit.

Weekly review

Level	Reading	Writing	Listening and speaking
■	Learner has not read the text well enough. Poor attention to detail. Requires more assistance in differentiating between facts and opinions.	Learner has difficulty in sequencing information.	Learner's digital presentation lacked sufficient content. Poor flow of content.
●	Learner reads well, paying careful attention to detail. Shows a good understanding of the difference between fact and opinion.	Learner has a good understanding of the sequencing of information.	Learner's digital presentation was clear and well-researched.
▲	Learner reads with excellent comprehension.	Learner completed the activity on sequencing extremely quickly and correctly.	Learner's presentation was extremely well-presented. It was well researched and well planned. Excellent content.

Week 2

Student's Book pages 71–77

Workbook pages 33–36

Student's Book pages 71–72

Reading and speaking

Write the words 'STANLEY YELNATS' on the board. Ask your class what a palindrome is. Explain that a palindrome is a word that reads the same, backwards and forwards and that the protagonist in Holes has the name 'Stanley Yelnats'. Let them play around with their own names to make up palindromic first and family names.

Remind the class that they read an extract from Holes in Unit 5. Read the blurb and explain that you are now going to read some more extracts from the same book.

Divide learners into pairs and instruct them to discuss the questions leading up to them reading the extract. Responses will vary.

1 and 2 Instruct learners to read the extract. Once they have done so, discuss how the author of the text has manipulated the reader by either challenging preconceived ideas or not revealing all the information about the plot and characters.

3 Tell learners that the next extract is a complete chapter.

Discuss the possible crimes Stanley could have committed. Write the suggestions on the board as they are suggested.

4 and 5 Divide learners into groups to discuss the questions. Encourage them to justify their responses.

Discuss the matter of consequences for negative behaviour. Ask the class to share their experiences of being punished. This will be an interesting and entertaining discussion as learners will have very strong opinions about the types of punishments they have experienced. Throughout the discussion, ask the question: Does the punishment fit the crime?

Instruct the groups to suggest possible punishments for the list of wrongdoings. Encourage the groups to share their responses with the rest of the class. Then discuss the following question: Is punishment the best way to modify bad behaviour?

Student's Book pages 73–74

Speaking and presenting

Introduce this task by referring to the reflections learners had done on their presentation activity earlier on in the theme. Write down positive points on one side of the board, and negative ones on the other. Explain that the success of the presentation task will depend on how well the group members work together.

Reinforce that not everyone has the same abilities or interests, but that does not mean that one person is any better than anyone else. This task gives learners the opportunity to focus on their strengths with a team goal in mind. Each learner will have a designated role to play and will be accountable to the group for the outcome of their respective responsibilities. Discuss the fact that effective communication skills include the ability to collaborate on a project.

Instruct learners to discuss the questions. These will guide their ideas for their final presentation.

Divide learners into groups and let each learner choose a role in the project. Give definite time lines so that the task does not drag on and lose momentum.

Stress the importance of the final presentation. Instruct learners to use the check list to bench mark their performance. Tell the class that they will be evaluating each other's presentations.

Give each group a copy of PCM 17: Group Evaluation. The groups will evaluate each other's presentations. This will be especially meaningful as learners have had to go through the same procedure and will have a very good insight of the value and success of each presentation.

After all the groups have presented, let learners again reflect on the task and compare it to the first presentation they did.

Student's Book page 75
Spelling and vocabulary

Answers
illogical; unemotional; inappropriate; irreplaceable; uneventful; misbehaving; unreal

Workbook page 33
Spelling

Answers
1 illegal; illiterate; displeased; imperfect; immoral; illegible' disjointed; unimpressed; incorrect; inconsistent; unhappy; unemotional; illegible; unfair; irregular; irresponsible; disconnected
2 Stanley was an inoffensive boy who has been unfairly accused of a crime he did not commit. It was impossible to prove his innocence. He misunderstood what the camp would be like. The judge was unimpressed with Stanley.

Student's Book pages 75–76
Reading

1 Instruct learners to read chapter 2 of *Holes* again, on Student's Book page 72. Discuss the questions.

It is important that learners constantly look for hidden clues in the texts they read.

2 Read and discuss the extract from the beginning of chapter 3.

Workbook pages 34–35
Reading

Example answers
Stanley is portrayed as a dangerous person which is why he is guarded so closely.
No, we assume this sort of person to be violent and unfeeling.
Our preconceived ideas are challenged by Stanley writing to his mother. We do not expect dangerous criminals to write to their mothers every week.
We learn that Stanley is a lonely boy.
We learn that Stanley is overweight, and that he is bullied.
Open question.

Student's Book page 76
Comprehension

Sample answers
a Summaries of the paragraphs:
- Stanley Yelnats was a passenger on a bus.
- He had personal belongings with him.
- The bus journey was extremely difficult.
- Stanley was a lonely boy.
- His teacher embarrassed him.
- Stanley was arrested later that day.
- Stanley watched the guard.

b 3rd Person – Limited
c He was timid and overweight
d Open question
e Open question
f Open question
g Open question

Extension

If your learners have access to the internet, they could watch the following video on bullying:
http://generator.acmi.net.au/library/media/game

Student's Book page 77

Grammar

Read through the notes. Use the questions as prompts to develop learners' understanding of how texts are structured.

Workbook page 36

Grammar

Answers
1
a consequently
b therefore
c therefore
d nevertheless
e however
2
a You can lie in the shade (if) you've been bitten by a yellow-spotted lizard.
b The Warden owns the shade (because) she's in charge of the camp.
c Stanley's hands were sore (as) he was not used to digging holes.
d Stanley felt confused (when) a sneaker fell out of the sky.
e No-one believed (that) he had not stolen the sneaker.
3 Open questions.

Support

Answers to PCM 18
1
when
After
begin
First
then
When
then
Finally
2 Open question.

Weekly review

Level	Reading	Listening and speaking
■	Learner has not engaged sufficiently with the extracts. Shows very little insight.	Learner showed little interest in the presentation task and made little effort to collaborate with the group.
●	Learner has attempted to engage actively with the texts. Has attempted to infer the author's intention.	Learner collaborated well with the group. Task was completed well. Good presentation.
▲	Learner has engaged fully and enthusiastically with the texts. Has developed insight into how authors manipulate the reader.	Learner showed complete commitment to the group task. Excellent presentation skills.

Week 3

Student's Book pages 77–81

Workbook pages 37–38

Student's Book page 77

Writing

Divide learners into pairs. Instruct them to create a set of open ended questions for an interview with Stanley Yelnats.

Workbook page 37

Writing

Give your learners the challenge of mimicking a published author's writing style.

- Let learners act out an interview with Stanley Yelnats, using the questions they wrote as a writing activity.

Student's Book page 78

Reading

The author of *Holes* creates suspense and interest by continuously giving clues about preceding events – events that have huge consequences on Stanley's life. We find out why Stanley is at Camp Green Lake *after* he gets there, and little by little, we find out more about what happened.

Explain what a flashback is. Alert learners that the extract they are about to read plays with flashbacks. Discuss how time as a concept is presented in the extract.

Student's Book page 79
Comprehension

Example answers
a 'Back at school, a bully named Derrick Dunne used to torment Stanley…
when the shoe hit him on the head.'
b The flashback makes a past event more 'immediate' so that it has more relevance in real time.
c A flashback is bring the past into the present. Telling about something that happened in the past keeps it in the past.
d Foreshadowing is a technique used to create expectation and even suspense. Flashbacks bring the past into the present.

Student's Book page 79
Grammar

Learners' responses will vary.

Student's Book page 79
Spelling

Work through the questions with the class.

Answers
1 A short vowel sound precedes the *-tch* sound in the words.
2 A two-letter vowel sound precedes the *-ch* sound.
3 It would be easiest for learners to learn the exceptions to the spelling rule to avoid confusion.

Student's Book page 80
Reading and listening

1 If possible, play the digital recording of the poem 'High Flight' or, alternatively, read it aloud to the class.

Example answers
2
a A pilot is overwhelmed by a sense of peace and freedom as he flies high above earth. He feels joy and delight and marvels at how this could even be.
b 'Oh, I have slipped the surly bonds of earth'
- surly
- Gravity keeps us anchored to the ground. It stops us from having the freedom to fly.

c
- The pilot is feeling immense joy and absolute freedom. He has no inhibitions. Metaphor

d
- Open question
- Cumulonimbus
- The sun's rays are streaming through the clouds.
- Personification and alliteration

e He says he has flown higher than larks and eagles.
f He says he has 'topped the windswept heights'
g Exhilaration
h Open question.

Student's Book page 81
Reading and writing

Explain what 'kennings' are. Write the following words on the board and ask your learners to suggest two-word descriptions to describe them:

- eagle
- motor bike
- space rocket
- school bag
- monkey.

Write all the suggestions for the different nouns underneath each other.

Workbook page 38
Writing

Let learners complete this exercise before they write their own Kennings.

Weekly review

Level	Reading	Writing
■	Learner has not been able to interpret the poem successfully. Shows minimal understanding of figurative language. Learner has also found it difficult to understand how flashbacks add value to a text.	Learner has shown very little understanding of a Kennings poem. Descriptions of the topic lack originality and creativity.
●	Learner has a good grasp of how to interpret a poem. Satisfactory understanding of figurative language. Learner shows a fair understanding of foreshadowing and flashbacks as writing techniques.	Learner has shown a good understanding of a Kennings poem. Some of the descriptions are delightful.
▲	Learner has an impressive ability to analyse poetry and is comfortable with figurative language. Learner also has an excellent understanding of the nuances created by foreshadowing and flashbacks.	Learner has shown an excellent understanding of a Kennings poem, with excellent descriptions that are entertaining and original.

Formal assessment 2

To assess the main learning objectives in Units 4, 5 and 6, have learners do Formal assessment 2 independently. Mark the assessment and record relevant assessment information.

Mark scheme

Question 1

A Open question. Possible answer: use of alliteration. (1)

B Phobia. (1)

C Rational fear is understandable. We understand the fear of snakes, for instance. Irrational fear is fear that makes no sense. (2)

D Own sentence. Must be in first person. Must indicate her fear. Must be ONE sentence. (A complex/compound sentence is acceptable.) (2)

E Own sentence. Must be in first person. Must indicate his lack of sympathy/scorn. Must be ONE sentence. (A complex/compound sentence is acceptable.) (2)

F No, this is not an informative text. It is a narrative. (1)

G Title, headings, sub-headings, factual, can have graphics, formal tone. (3)

Question 2
A (3)

	Correctly structured	Incorrectly structured
Paragraph 1	Correct	
Paragraph 2		Incorrect
Paragraph 3		Incorrect

Question 3
A (4)

- **1** Predicate
- **2** Subject
- **3** Adverbial phrase of place
- **4** Adverb of manner

Question 4
A Learners' responses will vary. Possible responses below. (4)

- The dinosaurs lived <u>in inhospitable places</u>.
- The dinosaurs moved <u>slowly</u>.
- The dinosaurs were <u>very</u> big.
- The dinosaurs moved <u>extremely</u> slowly.

Question 5
A (6)

Sally Spider said, "I don't know why people are so scared of me."

"I don't know why people are so scared of me," said Sally Spider.

"I," said Sally Spider, "don't know why people are so scared of me."

Question 6
A (5)

1 The house in Belize had a thatched roof with open doors and windows because it is extremely hot in a jungle.

2 Living in a jungle, one becomes used to all kinds of unwelcome visitors; however, the tarantula has to be the worst!

3 Henry doesn't mind spiders although they look scary.

4 The spider fell onto her bed and she screamed in panic.

5 We live in a jungle, so we're used to all kinds of unwelcome visitors.

Question 7
A (5)

- Praying mantises, staying very still, wait for their prey to pass by.
- The mossy frog is hard to spot because it looks just like a piece of moss.
- Never pick up a scorpion, for its sting could make you very ill.
- Wetas, living in New Zealand, are one of the world's largest insects.
- As they can live till they're 30 years old, Tarantulas are spider superstars.

Question 8
A (3)

The boy rushed home from school because he wanted to ride his new bike.(Conjunction)

The boy rushed home from school; he wanted to ride his new bike. (Semi colon)

The boy rushed home from school. He wanted to ride his new bike. (Full stop)

Unit 7 Stop!

Unit overview

The main focus of this unit is on persuasive techniques – learners will be writing both a persuasive and a balanced report and will also participate in a formal debate on a controversial topic. Learners will also extrapolate information from an infograph as well as interpret content in a fictional text. Time will also be spent on learning about verbs, and the use of connectives will be explored further as they play an important role in linking paragraphs in a persuasive text. Learners will learn the rule for spelling words with –dje sound, and will also learn how to apply the colon and semi colon in their writing.

Unit 7	Reading	Writing	Listening and speaking
Stop! Texts *Rhino facts*, non-fiction, formal and impersonal *Rhino poaching*, non-fiction infographics, journalistic writing *Zoos,* non-fiction, argument and discussion *Arguments for and against legalising trade in rhino products*, non-fiction, argument and discussion *The Leopard Poachers*, fiction, extended narrative	6R01 Articulate personal responses to reading, with close reference to the text. 6R02 Revise different word classes. 6Rx1 Distinguish between fact and opinion in a range of texts and other media. 6Rx2 Paraphrase explicit meanings based on information from more than one point in the text. 6Ri2 Look for implicit meanings, and make plausible inferences from more than one point in the text. 6Rw1 Comment on a writer's use of language, demonstrating awareness of its impact on the reader. 6Rw3 Analyse the success of writing in evoking particular moods, e.g. suspense. 6Rw4 Begin to show awareness of the impact of a writer's choices of sentence length and structure. 6Rw6 Discuss and express preferences in terms of language, style and themes. 6Rw8 Analyse how paragraphs and	6W03 Develop a personal handwriting style to write legibly, fluently and with increasing speed, choosing the writing implement that is best suited for a task. 6Wa1 Establish and maintain a clear viewpoint, with some elaboration of personal voice. 6Wa5 Write a balanced report of a controversial issue. 6Wa11 Argue a case in writing, developing points logically and convincingly. 6Wa12 Use different genres as models for writing. 6Wt3 Manage the development of an idea throughout a piece of writing, e.g. link the end to the beginning. 6Wt4 Use a range of devices to support cohesion within paragraphs. 6Wt5 Use connectives to structure an argument or discussion. 6Wp1 Use a wider range of connectives to clarify relationships between ideas, e.g. however, therefore,	6SL1 Express and explain ideas clearly, making meaning explicit and respond to guidance about, and feedback on, the quality of contributions. 6SL2 Use spoken language well to persuade, instruct or make a case, e.g. in a debate. 6SL3 Vary vocabulary, expression and tone of voice to engage the listener and suit the audience, purpose and context. 6SL5 Speak confidently in formal and informal contexts. 6SL6 Pay close attention in discussion to what others say, asking and answering questions to introduce new ideas. 6SL7 Help to move group discussion forward, e.g. by clarifying, summarising.

	chapters are structured and linked. 6Rw13 Identify uses of the colon, semi-colon, parenthetic commas, dashes and brackets. 6Rv1 Recognise key characteristics of a range of non-fiction text types. 6Rv3 Revise language conventions and grammatical features of different types of text. 6Rv5 Explore autobiography and biography, and first and third person narration. 6Rv6 Identify features of balanced written arguments. 6Rv7 Take account of viewpoint in a novel, and distinguish voice of author from that of narrator.	although. 6Ws2 Use correct choices when representing consonants, e.g. 'ck'/'k'/'ke'/'que'/'ch'; 'ch'/'tch'; 'j'/'dj'/'dje'. 6Ws7 Investigate meanings and spellings of connectives.	

Related resources

- Audio files: *Some rhino facts*; *The Leopard Poachers Extract 1*; *The Leopard Poachers Extract 2*; *The Leopard Poachers Extract 3*
- PCM 19: Persuasive essay A
- PCM 20: Persuasive essay B
- PCM 21: A balanced argument

Week 1

Student's Book pages 82–86

Workbook page 39

Introduction to the unit

Illegal trade and trafficking has been the topic of debates and forums internationally, so it is likely that your learners will have some understanding of this contentious issue. You could introduce the unit by discussing the advantages and disadvantages of hunting or even canned hunting.

Use the slideshow (or your own pictures) to discuss rhinos and where they are found.

Spend some time talking about the difference between hunting and poaching. In many African languages, for example, there is a word for hunting but no separate word for poaching as traditionally there was no law that allowed for hunting in some cases and not others.

Student's Book page 82

Reading and speaking

1 Instruct learners to read through the facts about rhinos and to share any additional information they may know.

2 Discuss the statistics on rhino poaching. It would be helpful if you were to write the three dates on the board in chronological order with the number of killings for each year underneath.

Student's Book pages 83–84

Comprehension

1 Draw learners' attention to the structure of the infograph. Instruct them to read the information it presents. Divide learners into small groups and let them discuss the answers to the questions before answering them independently.

Example answers
2
a A visual representation of information or data, e.g. as a chart or diagram.
b Statistics are used to describe groups of numbers/data that have been collected and interpreted
c Statistics lend authority and authenticity to an argument.
d Open question.
e Open question.
f Open question.
g Open question.
h Open question.
i Open question.
j Statistics can be used as a shock factor to jolt the reader's understanding of a topic. Statistics can be manipulated, so they need to be read and interpreted carefully.

3 Instruct learners to continue reading and interpreting the infographic material. In groups, let learners discuss the questions.

Example answers
4
a Hidden in carpets, furniture or in suitcases.
b Open question.
c The statement is telling a truth, so it is a fact. It is a fact that people believe that rhino are poached to order. This can be proved.
d Handles of Jambiya daggers, cure for life-threatening diseases, sign of wealth and status.
e Open question.
f Open question.

Student's Book page 85

Grammar

1 Draw learners' attention to the different rules for using semi colons. Once you have done this, let learners work independently to punctuate the sentences.

Answers
2
a The game rangers are working closely with the police; they need all the support they can get.
b Owners of game farms are always on the lookout for poachers and often employ their own security guards.
c Mark Benson, 23; Trevor Brown, 26; and Dirk Botha, 34; have been arrested for poaching.
d There is far more poaching taking place; consequently, many animals are in danger.
e Poachers struck again last night; however, I am sure they will be caught!

Read through the uses of the colon. Let learners complete the task independently.

Answers
3
a The following animals are endangered: the Black Rhino, Leatherback Turtle and the Mountain Gorilla.
b Pack the following for your trip: binoculars, a tent and mosquito repellent.
c There is only one solution: protect endangered animals.
d We plan to leave at 5:30.

Support

Play a game to reinforce using the semi colon to connect closely-related sentences. Divide learners into groups of four: Learner A, B, C and D. Learner A says a sentence aloud. Learner B says another sentence aloud, keeping to the general topic of the first sentence. If the two sentences can be connected with a semi colon, learner C claps his/her hands. If the sentences cannot be connected using a semi colon, learner C jumps up and down. Learner D then writes the sentences down. Learners then rotate.

Workbook page 39

Reading and thinking

The focus of the following reading task is to develop an understanding of how an author can manipulate the reader through the use of particular persuasive strategies. So, this activity will equip learners with the persuasive techniques that will help them tackle this unit.

Answers
1
Rhino are endangered. FACT
We have to stop poaching! OPINION
Poaching can be stopped. OPINION
Rhino cannot see well. FACT
It's everyone's duty to protect animals. OPINION

2

Persuasive technique	Definition/example
Emotive language	The poachers slaughtered the defenceless animals mercilessly!
Alliteration	Bullets battered the rhino's raw hide.
Own opinion	I believe that poachers should be locked up with no chance of parole.
Rhetorical question	Can you really stand by and watch a species become extinct?
Anecdotes	I once saw a rhino wallowing in a mud pool.
First person narrative	I believe that poaching can be stopped.
List of three	Poaching is cruel, unnecessary and barbaric!
Statistics	Since 2007, rhino poaching in South Africa has increased by 3000%.
Direct address	You know poaching is wrong!
Contrasting pairs	If you know it's wrong, make it right!
Repetition	If one rhino is endangered, all rhinos are endangered.

Student's Book page 86

Reading and writing

1 Instruct learners to read the essay, and to take note of the various persuasive techniques evident in the text. Draw learners' attention to the information boxes surrounding the text.

Support
Let the weaker learners complete PCM 19: Persuasive essay A

Extension
Challenge your stronger learners to complete PCM 20: Persuasive essay B. It is almost identical to PCM 19: Persuasive essay A, but does not have bolded sentences or phrases as prompts.

Answers to PCM 19 and PCM 20

> **Refer to an expert's opinion**
> According to Jane Healy, PhD, author of *Endangered Minds: Why Children Don't Think – and What We Can Do About It*,
> **Rhetorical questions**
> Is this what we want?
> **Alliteration**
> TV test tubes. TV teaches tiny tots…
> **Three items in a row**
> …numbed by canned laughter, ridiculous plots and cheesy characters?
> **Statistics**
> The average American child watches three hours a day of TV.
> **Speaking directly to the reader**
> So, do you want to disempower children by blocking their creativity and stunting their communication skills? You can do it!
> **Emotive language**
> Small wonder these young children are so confused!
> **Contrasting pairs**
> I'm not saying that children should never watch TV, but I do say that viewing time should be limited.

Weekly review

Level	Reading	Speaking
■	Learner has shown little ability to interpret visual data in infographic form. Learner is unable to identify techniques used in persuasive writing.	Learner has made minimal contributions to group discussions about poaching and illicit trading.
●	Learner has been able to extrapolate information from an infographic. This learner shows a satisfactory understanding of persuasive texts.	Learner has participated in group discussions about poaching and illicit trading.
▲	Learner has been able to extrapolate and interpret information taken from an infographic. This learner shows a clear understanding and appreciation of the nuances of persuasive texts.	Learner's contributions in group discussions on poaching and illicit trading have been extremely valuable.

Week 2

Student's Book pages 86–92

Student's Book pages 86–87

Writing

2 Instruct learners to reread the essay on the impact zoos have on animals in captivity. Tell them to focus on the structure of the paragraphs as well as the persuasive techniques. Instruct learners to work independently, or in pairs, to answer the questions.

Sample
a Topic sentence for each paragraph
- It is not certain whether zoos are beneficial to animals in captivity or not.
- Zoo animals are usually kept in terribly cramped enclosures and do not behave like their wild counterparts.
- Another problem with zoos is that a zoo is an unnatural environment that exposes animals to numerous dangers.
- Zoos do not help to protect endangered species.

b Connection of paragraphs and ideas
- Introduction ends with: Thirdly, **zoo animals** are exposed to many diseases and other dangers.
- Paragraph two begins: Zoo animals are usually kept…
- Paragraph three begins: Anther reason…
- Conclusion begins: In conclusion, therefore, it is…

c Anyone who supports zoos for breeding programmes, parents of young children

d Instruct learners to work in pairs for the last question and to **plan** an essay on a controversial topic. Use Workbook 2 Writing: How to write a persuasive essay to structure their planning.

Student's Book page 87

Speaking

Revise the different techniques used in persuasive writing and tell learners that these can also be used to great effect in debating. Revise the procedure for a debate and, if necessary, refer learners to Unit 1 page 6.

Read the points in the table, and expand on them in a general class discussion. Divide learners into teams and instruct them to do more extensive research on the topic. Debate the topic.

Student's Book page 88

Spelling

1 Instruct learners to examine the words in the three sets. Let them work in pairs to work out a strategy to learn how to spell the words.

2 Instruct learners to use the words in interesting sentences.

Student's Book page 89

Speaking

Read the introduction to the story with appropriate expression. Let learners discuss the questions about the reading, in pairs.

Example answers
a The author doesn't give any real context. Beginning with direct speech (Instructions).

b Strong verbs and descriptions – hissed, peered, nervously
c Action – dropped to the rocky ground

Student's Book pages 89–92
Reading and writing
1 Instruct learners to work in pairs or small groups and let them take turns to read parts of the extract to each other.

Example answers
2
a Sameer
b Open question.
c Open question.
d They were upwind
e Use of positive adjectives
f Possibly not. Direct speech allows us to become part of the conversation.
g Possibly not. 3rd person narrative distances the reader from the plot.

3 If possible, play the audiofile of the extract, or, alternatively, read the extract to the class. Encourage learners to read along, silently, from their books. Let learners discuss the answers to the questions in pairs.

Answers
4
a The leopard was hurt and had a wound on its leg.
b Open question.
c 'Pounded' gives a sense of urgency to the scene.
d He was in a rush and was not looking where he was going.

e Open question.
f People who buy goods illegally. Hunters need permits to shoot animals.
g Both texts mention poaching/centre around poaching.
h Open question.

5 Either play a recording of the next extract, or read it aloud to the class. Encourage learners to read along, silently, from their books. Before learners attempt the next set of questions, discuss the characteristics of different types of texts. Look through the Student's Book again, noting the different types of texts and their characteristics.

Sample answers
6
a Open question.
b Deciding to disobey their parents (Man *vs* man), facing the poachers (Man *vs* man), falling on the rocks (man *vs* environment)
c Deciding on whether to disobey their parents. Escaping from the poachers.
d By including so much detail, the writer takes greater control of the reader's interpretation of the text.
e End of Chapter one: Another second and both boys were gone. Beginning of Chapter two: Sameer and Ali clambered down the mountain.
The two sentences are closely connected – both focus on the two bows. The second chapter thus flows out of the first chapter.

Weekly review

Level	Writing	Speaking
■	Learner has not been able to apply characteristics of persuasive writing.	Learner's participation in a class debate was poor. Very little preparation made for a lack lustre argument.
●	Learner has successfully attempted to apply the characteristics of persuasive writing. Learner shows a good understanding of how to manipulate a reader.	Learner participated actively in a class debate.
▲	Learner has a thorough understanding of how to influence a reader through using persuasive writing techniques.	Learner's enthusiastic participation and excellent preparation ensured a commendable level of debating.

Week 3

Student's Book pages 92–93

Workbook pages 40–43

Workbook pages 40–41
Writing
Explain the difference between a persuasive text and a balanced argument. Stress that even though both sides of an argument are presented in a balanced argument, the writer still has the opportunity to present his/her point of view to the reader.

Discuss the difference in planning a persuasive text and a balanced text.

Student's Book page 92
Writing
1 Discuss whether people should be allowed to keep exotic animals like chimpanzees or tigers. Write down some of the discussion points on the board. Instead of learners drawing their own graphic organiser to plan their essay, let them use the template on Workbook page 40.

2 Guide learners through the tips for effective persuasive writing. Spend some time explaining the impact of using connectives to drive a balanced argument. Instruct learners to plan and then write the essay. They may have to do further research.

Differentiation
Support
Work closely with the weaker learners. Give them each a copy of PCM 21: A balanced argument, and help them to fill in sentences in the blank spaces, using the prompts as a guide.

Student's Book page 93
Grammar
Whilst learners can easily identify action verbs, they may struggle with linking verbs, as a linking verb can either be a being verb or a linking verb. Write the heading ACTION VERBS in capital letters on the far left of the board. Discuss the characteristics of action verbs. Write the heading LINKING VERBS on the far right of the board. Beneath this heading, draw two arrows pointing in different directions. Beneath one arrow, write being verbs. Beneath the other arrow, write linking verbs.

Explain that LINKING VERBS (being and linking) connect a noun to an **adjective** or another noun. For example: Ben is **happy**. Ben is my cousin. There is NO action.

Explain that being verbs show a state of being, and that the most common being verbs are: is, am, are, was, were, be, being, became.
Explain that sometimes a verb looks like it's an action verb, but it's actually a linking verb. For example: Flowers **smell** beautiful. Sally *smells* the flowers. If a verb can be replaced with 'is' or 'are', the verb is a linking verb.

Read through the notes.

Workbook pages 42–43
Grammar

Answers
1
a The poachers had been tracking the leopard for three hours.
b The boys saw the wounded animal.
c Arabian leopards are almost extinct.
d It was beautiful.
e The leopard had a beautiful coat.
f The poachers chased the boys angrily.
g Sameer and Ali felt frightened.
h They were also thirsty.
i Animals have to be protected from poachers.
j Save endangered animals!
2
The rifle shot boomed through the darkening forest just as Damien Mander arrived at his campfire after a long day training game ranger recruits in western Zimbabwe's Nakavango game reserve. His thoughts flew to Basta, a pregnant black rhinoceros and her two-year-old calf. That afternoon one of his rangers had discovered human footprints following the pair's tracks as Basta sought cover in deep bush to deliver the newest member of her threatened species.
Damien, a hard-muscled former Australian Special Forces sniper with an imposing menagerie of tattoos, including 'Seek & Destroy' in gothic lettering across his chest, swivelled his head, trying to place the direction of the shot. "There, near the eastern boundary," he pointed into the blackness. "Sounded like a .223," he said, identifying the position and calibre, a habit left over from 12 tours in Iraq. He and his rangers grabbed shotguns, radios, and medical kits and piled into two Land Cruisers. They roared into the night, hoping to cut off the shooter. The rangers rolled down their windows and listened for a second shot, which would likely signal Basta's calf was taken as well.
3 Open question
4 Open question

Weekly review

Level	Writing
■	Learner has very little idea of how to write a balanced argument. The argument flows poorly due to the incorrect use of connectives. Learner has very little understanding of verbs.
●	Learner has attempted to portray both sides of an argument. Good effort has been made to connect ideas and paragraphs. Learner has a fairly good understanding of action and linking verbs.
▲	Learner has written a beautifully balanced essay, and has been able to develop the argument sensible, ending with a believable conclusion. Learner has an excellent understanding of the difference between action and linking verbs.

Unit 8 I spy

Unit overview

This unit deals with three texts: a biography on Virginia Hall, an infographic on spying, and a narrative by Benjamin Zephaniah about a young refugee boy. Learners will create their own infographic, write a letter, and an autobiographical account of an imaginary event in character. There is a strong human interest in this unit, and many opportunities for discussions will present themselves. In addition, learners will prepare and give a formal oral presentation. The spelling lessons concentrate on the prefixes -ad, -al, -af and -ap, as well as the rules for doubling consonants. Grammar lessons will reinforce knowledge of the active and passive voice as well as the different tenses of verbs.

Unit 8	Reading	Writing	Listening and speaking
I spy Texts *Virginia Hall: World War II Spy*, non-fiction, biography *Refugee Boy*, fiction, extended narrative with flashbacks	6R01 Articulate personal responses to reading, with close reference to the text. 6R02 Revise different word classes. 6R03 Develop familiarity with the work of established authors and poets, identifying features which are common to more than one text. 6Rx2 Paraphrase explicit meanings based on information from more than one point in the text. 6Ri1 Consider how the author manipulates the reaction of the reader, e.g. how characters and settings are presented. 6Ri2 Look for implicit meanings, and make plausible inferences from more than one point in the text. 6Rw1 Comment on a writer's use of language, demonstrating awareness of its impact on the reader. 6Rw11 Explore use of active and passive verbs within a sentence. 6Rv1 Recognise key characteristics of a range of non-fiction text types. 6Rv2 Understand the conventions of standard English usage in different forms of writing.	6W01 Continue to learn words, apply patterns and improve accuracy in spelling. 6W02 Use handwriting and IT effectively, making appropriate choices of presentation, to prepare writing for publication. 6W03 Develop a personal handwriting style to write legibly, fluently and with increasing speed, choosing the writing implement that is best suited for a task. 6Wa1 Establish and maintain a clear viewpoint, with some elaboration of personal voice. 6Wa2 Develop some imaginative detail through careful use of vocabulary and style. 6Wa3 Explore definitions and shades of meaning and use new words in context. 6Wa6 Develop skills of writing biography and autobiography in role. 6Wa7 Adapt the conventions of the text type for a particular purpose. 6Wa12 Use different genres as models for writing.	6SL1 Express and explain ideas clearly, making meaning explicit and respond to guidance about, and feedback on, the quality of contributions. 6SL4 Structure talk to aid a listener's understanding and engagement. 6SL5 Speak confidently in formal and informal contexts. 6SL6 Pay close attention in discussion to what others say, asking and answering questions to introduce new ideas. 6SL7 Help to move group discussion forward, e.g. by clarifying, summarising. 6SL8 Prepare, practise and improve a spoken presentation or performance. 6SL10 Reflect on variations in speech, and appropriate use of standard English.

	6Rv3 Revise language conventions and grammatical features of different types of text. 6Rv4 Compare the language, style and impact of a range of non-fiction writing. 6Rv5 Explore autobiography and biography, and first and third person narration. 6Rv7 Take account of viewpoint in a novel, and distinguish voice of author from that of narrator. 6Rv8 Begin to develop awareness that the context for which the writer is writing and the context in which the reader is reading can impact on how the text is understood.	6Wt2 Use paragraphs, sequencing and linking them appropriately to support overall development of the text. 6Wt5 Use connectives to structure an argument or discussion. 6Wp5 Punctuate speech and use apostrophes accurately. 6Ws4 Develop knowledge of word roots, prefixes and suffixes, including recognising variations, e.g. *im, in, ir, il; ad, ap, af, al* and knowing when to use double consonants. 6Ws5 Know how to transform meaning with prefixes and suffixes. 6Ws6 Explore word origins and derivations and the use of words from other languages.	

Related resources

- Audio files: *Virginia Hall Extract 1*; *Virginia Hall Extract 2*; *Refugee Boy – Ethiopia*; *Refugee Boy – Eritrea*; *Refugee Boy Extract 3*; *Refugee Boy Extract 4*
- PCM 22: Verbs – present tense
- PCM 23: Verbs – past tense
- PCM 24: Verbs – future tense
- PCM 25: Prepared oral planning sheet

Week 1

Student's Book pages 94–101

Workbook pages 44–48

Introduction to the unit

World War I involved most countries in some way and lead to many deaths. In 2014, an exhibition was held in London to highlight the fact that over 880 000 soldiers from the UK and its allies died during the war. This exhibition involved making a red ceramic poppy for each person and planting this in the moat around the Tower of London, in the UK. Millions of people visited the exhibition and the poppies were sold to raise funds to help modern day servicemen and women.

If possible, display a photograph of the exhibtion and discuss the photograph and the impact of the display. How does making an exhibition like this one make people aware of the effects of war?

Spend some time talking about the topic of war to gauge learners' knowledge of the topic.

Student's Book page 94

Speaking

1 Let learners discuss the questions in small groups. If time allows, let the groups share their views.

Student's Book page 94

Reading

Briefly explain the role Winston Churchill played in World War II. If possible, play a short extract from one of his speeches. (Search online.)

Ask learners what they know about spies.

Workbook page 44

Spelling and vocabulary

Answers

Spy Language	Definition
brush pass	a brief moment where two agents 'meet' and quickly exchange information, documents, and/or equipment.
bug	a secret listening device that is used to listen in on conversations while not being in the same room.
burned	when a person notices that you are tracking their moves
undercover	the role that an agent plays to hide that he's actually a spy
dead drop	a special location that is used to get information (or objects) from one spy to another spy, without the need for the spies to meet.
microdot	a text or an image that has been reduced in size so that it's just about 1mm in diameter, and usually circular in shape.
mole	an agent that has penetrated into an organization.
safehouse	used by spies to safely hide from the enemy
shadowing	spy talk for secretly following someone
sleeper	an agent, who's living in a foreign country as a citizen. Unlike most other agents, the agent doesn't involve him or herself in spying activity until he or she is activated for an operation.

Workbook page 45

Grammar

Answers

Working **undercover** as an office cleaner, the agent hid a **bug** behind the painting in the politician's office. The politician was suspected of being a **mole**, and the agent's instructions were to find out whether this was so. The politician had handed a small package to a suspicious-looking individual – was it a **brush pass** or just a co-incidence? Only time would tell. Just to be sure, the agent planned to **shadow** the politician and, if necessary, activate a **sleeper** to keep track of the politician's movements. He would leave all the necessary instructions and information at the **dead drop**. It was just a matter of time – but precious time, as the country's safety was at stake!

Student's Book page 95

Comprehension

Instruct learners to read the extract silently. Let learners discuss the questions in pairs before writing the answers independently in their books.

Sample answers
a The more information a country has, the better it can plan to win a war.
b A spy's task is to gather information without the enemy knowing and pass it back to his/her commanders.
c Open question.
d Money, fame, dissatisfaction with their government, blackmail
e Satisfaction
f Open question.

Thinking deeper

Learners take part in their own discussion, but should focus on disability and the fact that having a wooden leg (not a modern prosthetic one) would have made certain things quite difficult.

Student's Book pages 96–97

Reading and speaking

Instruct learners to scan the next extract and to tell a partner what they notice about the characteristics of the text. Ask random learners to share their observations. Possible responses would be: narrative, biography, third person.

Comprehension

Sample answers
a France surrendered to Germany in June 1940, and Hitler's army prepared to move into Paris.
b She went to the US Embassy where she was offered a job.
c Discrimination against women/ her wooden leg made her unsuitable for an active job (or so it was believed.)
d She volunteered her services to the SOE because she wanted to rejoin the fight against evil (Germany), but America was not at war with Germany, so she had to find another way to make her mark.
e Open question.
f To set Europe ablaze by waging an undercover war against the Germans who had occupied France.
g She was female, Non-British, an expert in languages and comfortable with living in a foreign country.
h Open question.
i No discrimination in the tasks they would be doing.
j To prepare them fully for all eventualities.
k Parachuting – wooden leg
l She could not be secretly dropped into an area.
m They had to be prepared to die rather than give information away in an interrogation which is why they were issued with cyanide pills.

Workbook pages 45–46

Reading and thinking

1 Discuss the types of training the spies received. Tell learners that they are going to pretend to be spies and are to crack the coded words.

Answers
2
iodra – radio
municomticaons – communications
lugergnil – gruelling
meney – enemy
gnunadh – handgun
lengsellcha – challenges
viruslav – survival
chteurapa – parachute

Student's Book page 98

Spelling and vocabulary

Thinking deeper

The prefix **ad-** has the same meaning as *al-*, *af-* and *ap-*.

1 Instruct learners to look up the meanings of each word before they write the words in sentences in their books.

2 Remind learners about the definitions of root words, prefixes and suffixes. Write the word 'responsible' on the board. Ask a random learner which prefix should be added to the word to turn it into a negative. Join *ir-* to the beginning of the word. Draw learners' attention to the double *rr*. Instruct them to apply this to the prefixes and root words in the table.

Answers
affirm, approximate, alleviate, apprehend, allow

To make spelling more appealing, turn learning words into a game. The workbook activity is suitable for any extract in the Student's Book. Alternatively, give learners a list of words to use for the activity.

Workbook page 47

Spelling and vocabulary

Open questions.

Student's Book pages 99–100

Grammar

Using a timeline helps to visually 'plot' changes in time.

Simple tense	The action happens at the moment. It starts and finishes.
Progressive tense	The action is happening and does not stop. The verbs end in *-ing*
Perfect tense	Use the perfect tense to describe an experience.

Perfect tense seems to be the most challenging concept for learners to understand. Give as many examples as necessary to reinforce the different tenses. Use the verb 'walk' as a starting point. Write the following on the board:

Simple	I walked.	I walk.	I will walk.
Continuous	I was walking.	I am walking.	I will be walking.
Perfect	I had walked.	I have walked.	I will have walked.

Replace 'walk' with various other action verbs.

Answers
1
a moved
b decided, sending
c did, was
d used, pick, coming
e captured, forced
f used

g prearranged, trusted
h worked, failed, used, confirmed

2
a The man was spying for his country. (Progressive present tense)
b The man will be spying for his country. (Progressive future tense)
c Virginia Hall had spied for the British Government. (Past perfect tense)
d Virginia Hall has spied for the British Government. (Present perfect tense)
e Virginia Hall will have spied for the British Government. (Future perfect tense)

Support
Make copies of PCMs 22, 23 and 24 for each learner who needs extra support.

Answers to PCM 22
1
a is having
b drinks, drank
c is raining, do not have
d do not
e is making, is blowing
f telling
g goes
h am spending, visit
i asking
j are you speaking

2
a has been
b have played
c have had
d Have you seen
e has been
f am taking
g have had
h have been irritating
i has been raining
j have not been feeling

3
a is bringing
b often listens
c are writing
d is baking
e gives
f is reading
g grows
h are building
i drinks
j is running

Answers to PCM 23
1
a enjoyed
b visited
c played
d travelled
e phoned
f walked
g liked
h stopped
i Listened
j watched

2
a was skating
b was walking
c was riding
d was studying
e were dancing
f was peeling
g were baking
h was sleeping

3 Open question

Answers to PCM 24
1
a Open question. e.g. So at 5.55pm I'll quickly make some popcorn.
b Open question.
c Open question.
d Open question.

2
a will have written
b will not have forgotten
c will have decorated
d will have been
e not have made

3
I was going to take a taxi home last night, but my friend offered me a lift instead.
I was to drive to town, but my car had no petrol.
We were going to play tennis, but then it stated to rain, so we played scrabble instead.
Dan was going to eat the cake, but he decided on an apple instead.
They were going to watch a movie, but they decided to go for a walk instead.

4
(Will / Going to / Present Continuous / Simple Present)
1 What are you going to do when you grow up?
I am going to be an acrobat in a circus.
2 I haven't seen my cousin for a long time but I'm sure I will recognise him.
3 I need some money to buy a shirt.
I will give you some.
4 I got the plane tickets. I going to fly on Tuesday.
5 Have you got any plans for the summer?
Yes, we are going to India in June.

Student's Book page 100
Reading and speaking
Remind learners about the characteristics of an infographic. Ask random learners to list the characteristics of dialogues, letters, short stories, poems, plays and information texts.

Answers
a Spying
b Training activities of spies, equipment used by spies, messages
c Open question

Workbook page 48

Writing

Let learners create their own infographic using the template.

Student's Book page 101

Speaking

Revise the criteria for a prepared oral. Write these on the board, and if necessary, model these for learners. Make a copy of PCM 25: Prepared oral planning sheet. This template will assist learners to structure their thoughts and information. Emphasise that the paragraphs need to be connected properly so that the information flows smoothly. If necessary, let learners do extra research.

Extension

Let learners create a visual/digital presentation to support their prepared oral.

Student's Book page 101

Writing

1 Give learners an opportunity to discuss Virginia Hall's life and experiences. Divide them into small groups and instruct them to pretend to be Virginia Hall and to create a short scene on one of the following topics:

- Virginia Hall thinks she is being followed
- Virginia Hall tries to recruit a new spy
- Virginia Hall needs to persuade someone to hide her
- A German officer suspects a woman is a spy
- Virginia Hall speaks to another spy

Let learners write their own autobiographical account of an imaginary event.

Weekly review

Level	Reading	Writing	Speaking
■	Learner has very little understanding of an infographic. Learner has not been able to create own infographic satisfactorily.	Learner has put little effort into writing an autobiographical account in character.	Learner has not put enough effort into the prepared oral. Poor content, sloppy structure and weak presentation.
●	Learner has shown a good understanding of an infographic and has been able to translate this insight into a satisfactory infographic.	Learner has written a pleasing autobiographical account in character.	Learner worked carefully and structured a good oral. God presentation.
▲	Learner has a very clear understanding of an infographic. This has enabled learner to create an outstanding infographic.	Learner has written an excellent autobiographical account in character.	Learner structured an excellent oral. Content flowed smoothly. Accurate content with signs of extra research. Engaging presentation.

Week 2

Student's Book pages 101–104

Workbook pages 48–50

Introduction

This section has a refugee theme. If possible, source news articles on refugees that you could either print and display, or project on a screen. It would be wise to do your own research prior to the lesson.

Background information on refugees

According to the UNHCR, the practice of granting asylum to people fleeing persecution in foreign lands is one of the earliest hallmarks of civilization. References to it have been found in texts written 3,500 years ago, during the blossoming of the great early empires in the Middle East such as the Hittites, Babylonians, Assyrians and ancient Egyptians.

Over three millennia later, protecting refugees was made the core mandate of the UN refugee agency, which was set up to look after refugees, specifically those waiting to return home at the end of World War II.

The 1951 Refugee Convention spells out that a refugee is someone who "owing to a well-founded fear of being persecuted for reasons of race, religion, nationality, membership of a particular social group or political opinion, is outside the country of his nationality, and is unable to, or owing to such fear, is unwilling to avail himself of the protection of that country."

Since then, UNHCR has offered protection and assistance to tens of millions of refugees, finding durable solutions for many of them. Global migration patterns have become increasingly complex in modern times, involving not just refugees, but also millions of economic migrants. But refugees and migrants, even if they often travel in the same way, are fundamentally different, and for that reason are treated very differently under modern international law.

Migrants, especially economic migrants, choose to move in order to improve the future prospects of themselves and their families. Refugees have to move if they are to save their lives or preserve their freedom. They have no protection from their own state – indeed it is often their own government that is threatening to persecute them. If other countries do not let them in, and do not help them once they are in, then they may be condemning them to death – or to an intolerable life without sustenance and without rights.

Conduct a general discussion on refugees.

Workbook pages 48–49

Vocabulary

Answers
2

Does a migrant worker always live in the same place?	no
Do countries have to offer refugees sanctuary?	no
Is a migrant a refugee?	no
Do refugees get sent into exile?	no
Can refugees return home?	no
Are refugees homeless?	yes
Are refugees vagrants?	no
Can refugees be fugitives?	yes

Student's Book page 101

Writing

2 Instruct the groups to discuss the questions before holding a whole class follow up.

Answers
a A refugee has a well-founded fear of being persecuted for reasons of race, religion, nationality, membership of a particular social group or political opinion
b Open question
c Migrants, especially economic migrants, choose to move in order to improve the future prospects of themselves and their families. Refugees have to move if they are to save their lives or preserve their freedom.

Student's Book pages 102–103

Reading and speaking

Display a map of Eritrea and Ethiopia and make sure that learners have a clear understanding of each country's geographical location. Then ask learners questions about children who have parents of different nationalities – should this be a problem, what are the benefits, what are the negatives? Hold a brief class discussion.

Instruct learners to read the prologue.

In small groups, let them discuss the questions relating to the extract they have just read.

Answers
2
a Identical information
b One side is black, the other: white. Each extract has a different country.
c Own opinion
d Own opinion
e By mirroring the racism, and making the conflict happen in the same way to the same people, the writer is showing that the discrimination is happening throughout the world.
f Open question.

Student's Book pages 103–104

Reading and speaking

As an introduction to the reading activity, ask learners whether people get judged by the way they speak. Briefly discuss.

1 Instruct learners to read the extract.

Answers
2
a An accent that is 'put on'.
b Open question.

c Open question.
d Open question.

Workbook page 50
Writing

Answers
1 a He taught me some new words
b I'm not going with you.
c We were just playing a game!
d He should have taken more care!
e Give me those sweets.
f I have no money.
2
a A cute baby
b Improve your English
c Search the room
d He lacks sophistication
e An obvious error
f A person who thinks they are more intelligent and more important than they really are
3
a Wrote
b Fought
c Flew
d Spoke

Student's Book page 104
Writing

Sample answer
'Here you are, sir,' said the driver, 'the Palace Hotel. What a lovely little house" Alem and his father couldn't understand what he said, but they knew that they had arrived.
'I beg your pardon?' By now Alem's father had dropped his pseudo-posh accent.
The taxi driver pointed to the house and spoke louder and slower. 'That is a lovely little house, I said.'
'Oh, yes,' replied Alem's father as he raised the corners of his lips a tiny little bit in order to represent a smile. 'It is a nice building. How much money shall I pay you?'
'Eighteen pounds and fifty pence, sir.'

Weekly review

Level	Reading	Writing	Speaking
■	Learner shows very little insight and is not able to show a satisfactory understanding of the author's intentions.	Learner has little understanding of standard English	Learner has little understanding of standard English.
●	Learner has a satisfactory understanding of the author's intention.	Learner has a satisfactory understanding of standard English.	Learner has a good understanding of dialects and standard English.
▲	Learner has an excellent understanding of the author's intention in his writing.	Learner has an excellent understanding of standard English.	Learner has an excellent understanding of how people are judged by their accents and vocabulary.

Week 3

Student's Book pages 104–108

Student's Book pages 104–105
Reading

Instruct learners to read the extract. Take feedback from different learners about their response to the text.

Student's Book page 105
Comprehension

Answers
a Alem asked, "What is this all about?" This shows he is confused.
b The author is showing that refugees have no freedom in their new countries. This shows that their lives have not improved.
c His father was a qualified person who had been in a good job and always proud to have earned every penny he had, but now was reduced to what amounted to living off aid.
d To show that these people were not wanting hand-outs, but wanted to be productive members of society.
e His father saw him silently shake his head in disgust as they slowly shuffled down the line.
f This reinforces how disempowered the refugees are, and what little value they have in their new countries. The refugees are forced to wait in long queues, yet there are bored cahiers available who *could* assist them.

g He was angry that his father, an intelligent, educated man, was reduced to living off aid.
h This shows that the refugees were not useless, but were being forced to be dependent.
i Open question.
j Refugees are valuable people who want to be productive.
k Open question.
l Open question – people can pretend that they do not discriminate against others who may be different to them, but when these people become close neighbours, their viewpoints can change.

Student's Book page 106
Speaking and writing
1 Discuss the choice that Alem's parents made. Let learners choose their topic and then work in groups to brainstorm content for their letters.

2 Remind learners of the structure of a letter and instruct them to write a letter in the role of Alem.

Student's Book pages 106–107
Spelling
Write the word 'plan' on the board. Ask a random learner to read the word aloud. Ask another learner whether the vowel sound is long or short.

Write the word 'begin' on the board. Ask another learner to read the word aloud. Repeat the word, and emphasis the stressed syllable.

Explain that one syllable words with short sounding vowels and words that end with a stressed short syllable double the last consonant before adding a suffix.

Read through the lists and ask a learner to explain why the list with words having long vowel sounds does not follow the same rule.

Student's Book pages 107–108
Grammar
1 Tell learners to study the table. Revise and discuss the differences between active and passive voice.

Answers
2
a The refugee wrote the story of his life.
b Many people have signed a petition in support of asylum seekers.
c The government is helping the refugees.
3
a The story of his life was written by the refugee.
b A petition in support of asylum seekers has been signed by many people.
c The refugees have been helped by the government.

Level	Reading	Writing
■	Learner has little insight of the text and is not able to interpret the text adequately.	Learner's letter is poorly structured and has insufficient/superficial content.
●	Learner has a good insight of the text and interprets the text well.	Learner's letter is correctly structured and has sufficient and appropriate content.
▲	Learner shows an outstanding insight of the text and shows this in the way the text is interpreted.	Learner's letter is correctly structured and has outstanding content.

Unit 9 Sporting chance

Unit overview

This unit deals with two very different texts – an extract from Beth Tweddle's autobiography and a ballad by Alfred Noyes, *The Highwayman*. Learners will be required to develop their inferential skills through the questions they will be required to answer and the activities they will complete. Listening and speaking skills are also the focus of this unit, with learners pretending to be sports commentators and reading aloud. Learners will learn the value of using the dash in their writing, will write complex sentences and direct speech. They will work with unstressed vowels and use suffixes to change classes of words.

Unit 9	Reading	Writing	Listening and speaking
Sporting chance Texts *Becoming an Olympic Gymnast*, non-fiction, autobiography *The Highwayman*, poem with imagery	6R01 Articulate personal responses to reading, with close reference to the text. 6R02 Revise different word classes. 6R03 Develop familiarity with the work of established authors and poets, identifying features which are common to more than one text. 6Ri1 Consider how the author manipulates the reaction of the reader, e.g. how characters and settings are presented. 6Ri2 Look for implicit meanings, and make plausible inferences from more than one point in the text. 6Rw2 Explore proverbs, sayings and figurative expressions. 6Rw3 Analyse the success of writing in evoking particular moods, e.g. suspense. 6Rw9 Read and interpret poems in which meanings are implied or multilayered. 6Rw10 Explore how poets manipulate and play with words and their sounds.	6W01 Continue to learn words, apply patterns and improve accuracy in spelling. 6Wa1 Establish and maintain a clear viewpoint, with some elaboration of personal voice. 6Wa2 Develop some imaginative detail through careful use of vocabulary and style. 6Wa3 Explore definitions and shades of meaning and use new words in context. 6Wa4 Use the styles and conventions of journalism to write reports on events. 6Wa5 Write a balanced report of a controversial issue. 6Wa7 Adapt the conventions of the text type for a particular purpose. 6Wa12 Use different genres as models for writing. 6Wp2 Develop grammatical control of complex sentences, manipulating them for effect. 6Wp4 Develop increasing accuracy in using punctuation effectively to mark out	6SL1 Express and explain ideas clearly, making meaning explicit and respond to guidance about, and feedback on, the quality of contributions. 6SL2 Use spoken language well to persuade, instruct or make a case, e.g. in a debate. 6SL3 Vary vocabulary, expression and tone of voice to engage the listener and suit the audience, purpose and context. 6SL4 Structure talk to aid a listener's understanding and engagement. 6SL5 Speak confidently in formal and informal contexts. 6SL8 Prepare, practise and improve a spoken presentation or performance. 6SL9 Convey ideas about characters in drama in different roles and scenarios through deliberate choice of speech, gesture and movement. 6SL10 Reflect on variations in speech, and appropriate use of standard English.

		6Rw12 Understand changes over time in words and expressions and their use. 6Rw13 Identify uses of the colon, semi-colon, parenthetic commas, dashes and brackets. 6Rv1 Recognise key characteristics of a range of non-fiction text types. 6Rv3 Revise language conventions and grammatical features of different types of text. 6Rv5 Explore autobiography and biography, and first and third person narration.	the meaning in complex sentences. 6Wp5 Punctuate speech and use apostrophes accurately. 6Ws3 Further investigate spelling rules and exceptions, including representing unstressed vowels. 6Ws4 Develop knowledge of word roots, prefixes and suffixes.	

Related resources

- Audio files: *Becoming an Olympic Gymnast – Prologue*; *Becoming an Olympic Gymnast Extract 2*; *The Highwayman Part One*; *The Highwayman Part Two*
- PCM 26: Unstressed vowels

Week 1

Student's Book pages 109–115

Workbook pages 51–54

Introduction to the unit
Introduce the unit by discussing a recent sports match that some of learners will have played at school. Steer the discussion to the challenges learners face in balancing school work with sporting commitments.

Student's Book page 109

Listening and speaking
Divide your class into mixed 'interest' groups, so that learners who don't enjoy sport can share their opinions and insights with those who do. Remind your class of modern learning principles – that everyone has an equal voice if a collaborative effort is to be successful.

Instruct learners to discuss the questions preceding the text. It is important that they understand the meaning of 'a sporting chance', (an even or fair opportunity for success).

Discuss the implications of not having a sporting chance – quota systems, discrimination and other ideas learners may raise.

Student's Book pages 109–111

Reading
As learners will be reading aloud to each other, either have mixed ability groups containing at least one fluent reader or group the readers according to their reading abilities. By doing the latter, you will have more opportunities to assist struggling/reluctant readers.

Prior to them reading, instruct learners to take note of the headings, photographs and captions whilst they read.

Student's Book page 111

Comprehension

Answers
a Autobiographical. Written in the first person.

b Open question.
c Headings, photos with captions
d 'I didn't deserve to be there
e Top achievers
f She discovered her aptitude for the sport
g She was 'rewarded' for doing something that came naturally. She was completely comfortable.
h Amanda Reddin knew exactly what Beth Tweddle would be experiencing as she was a top gymnast herself.
i Open question.
j Open question.

Ask learners if any of them are fans of particular sportsmen or women. Write these names on the board. Discuss, briefly, the achievements of some of the sportsmen identified by the class. Then ask whether they (or their parents!) have ever wanted to give advice to a sportsman.

Workbook page 51
Reading
This activity is based on the premise of Twitter – a free social networking microblogging service that allows registered members to broadcast short posts called tweets. Each tweet can be no longer than 140 characters. Learners don't have to know anything about Twitter to complete the task.

Student's Book page 112
Spelling
Explain the concept of unstressed vowels

Support
PCM 26: Unstressed vowels

Answers
difference
deafening
generous
interested
general
miserable
different
jewellery
offering
secretary
dictionary
primary
literacy
boundary
stationary
voluntary
library

Extension
If your learners have access to internet, let them log in to the spellzone spelling website for fun activities to reinforce the unstressed vowels concept. Alternatively you can download free activities from the site to use as worksheets.

Student's Book pages 112–113
Reading
1 Instruct learners to read the text aloud in small groups. You may wish to change your grouping strategy this time.

Answers to comprehension questions
2
a Open question.
b Open question.
c Open question.
d Gymnastics follows laws and rules. It's right or it's wrong. Maths is the same.
e Open question.
f She means that she lost her focus
g Although they were strict about me getting my homework done, they also made sure I still had a good set of friends around me and I didn't separate myself off too much.

Student's Book page 114
Grammar
Remind learners about the dash and its function. Refer back to Unit 1 if you need to revise the concept in more detail.

Answers
1
a My favourite piece of apparatus – the bars – is what I've always been good at.
b I'm happy to swing around like a monkey – I have no fear of it.
c I have a lot to keep me busy – practising, studying and socialising with friends!
d My coach says I'm full of energy before a competition – I'm desperate to show everyone what I can do!
e I had a dream from when I was very young – that I was going to win gold!
2 Open question.

Student's Book pages 114–115
Comprehension
Explore the content of the graph with the class.

Answers
a Being awarded an MBE in 2010
b Open question.

c 2008 – won gold medal, 2006 – World title at World Championships, 2002 – won Gold. She won these competitions
d 2008 she fell during the bars qualification at the World championships
e Beth Tweddle experiences success which shows that she never gives up.

Workbook pages 52–53
Reading and writing
This is a good point to complete the 'Happiness graph'.

Student's Book page 115
Writing
With mobile phones being so advanced and accessible, taking photographs is part of everyday life. Discuss the value of documenting experiences photographically. Let learners complete the activity on their own or in pairs. Share some of the captions with the class and discuss what makes a good caption.

Workbook pages 53–54
Writing
Complete the scrapbook activity in the Workbook.

Weekly review

Level	Reading	Writing
■	Learner has not made a significant connection with the text. Responses to the Twitter reading activity are disappointing.	Learner made very little effort to create a 'scrapbook' page.
●	Learner has made a good connection with the text. Answers to comprehension questions show a clear understanding of the text.	Learner created an interesting 'scrapbook' page.
▲	Learner has shown an excellent understanding of the text. 'Tweets' written as a comprehension exercise were intuitive and sensible.	Learner's scrapbook page was carefully crafted with interesting detail.

Week 2
Student's Book pages 115–117

Student's Book page 115
Speaking
If possible, play the recording of a sports commentator. Alternatively, record a sports event and play a short extract to the class. Otherwise, instruct learners to watch a sports event prior to the lesson.

Discuss the action they were listening to/watching.

Play the recording again. This time, tell learners to focus on the commentator.

Discuss how the commentator keeps the unseen audience engaged. Discuss the use of emotive language.

1 Divide learners into small groups to discuss the questions.

2 Instruct learners to prepare and practise and then present their own commentary of an imaginary sports event. Let learners close their eyes as they listen to each other's commentaries.

Support
Let the shyer learners record their commentaries digitally and then play this recording to the class.

Student's Book page 116
Listening and reading
Before reading the ballad of the Highwayman to the class, give some historical background to the poem.

Historical background on highwaymen
(http://www.localhistories.org/highwaymen.html)

The idea of robbing people while they travel along roads is a very old one. In the Middle Ages there were plenty of outlaws ready to rob travellers. However the 'golden age' of highwaymen was the 17th century and 18th century. At that time trade and commerce were increasing and there were many well-to-do travellers. However Britain was still a pre-industrial country. The population was small and there were vast areas of forest and other countryside where highwaymen could lie in wait. The invention of the flintlock pistol early in the 17th century also made life easy for highwaymen. Furthermore Britain did not have a professional police force, which made it harder to catch them. The most dangerous roads where those around London.

There is a popular image of the highwayman as a gentleman and surprisingly some highwaymen were from quite wealthy backgrounds. Perhaps it was an exciting way of life being a highwayman but it was usually a short one – most were caught and hanged before they were 35.

Furthermore sometimes the travellers fought back. Many stagecoaches carried armed guards and some passengers carried pistols. There were also large rewards for anyone who could capture a highwayman and bring him to justice. Most highwaymen were eventually caught and hanged. Afterwards their body was sometimes hanged on a frame called a gibbet as a warning to others.

However from the end of the 18th century policing of the highways greatly improved and by the 1830s the age of the highwayman was over.

The most infamous highwayman is Dick Turpin. Although he is sometimes depicted as a dashing figure Turpin was actually a callous thug. He was born in 1705 in Essex. Turpin served an apprenticeship as a butcher but he soon turned to crime. At first Turpin tried smuggling and rustling livestock. Later Turpin joined a gang of robbers north of London. (They robbed people in their homes). Later he became a highwayman in the same area. Turpin eventually moved to York where he lived under the name John Palmer. However he was arrested in October 1738 after he shot a gamecock and the authorities soon realized who they were dealing with. Turpin was tried and then hanged in April 1739. Legally Turpin was hanged for horse stealing.

Not all highwaymen were men! There were also highway women. Among them were Joan Bracey, who was hanged in 1685. Other infamous highway women were Mary Frith, known as Moll Cutpurse and Catherine Ferrers.

Briefly give learners an outline of the first part of the poem. If possible, play the first part of the digital recording to the class. Alternatively, read it to your class, yourself. Instruct learners to read the text as they listen to it being read aloud.

Student's Book page 117
Comprehension

Answers
a Summaries of the verses
- A highwayman went riding on a cold, cloudy night
- He was beautifully dressed.
- He went to meet his lover, Bess, the landlord's daughter.
- Tim, the ostler heard them arrange to meet later and felt jealous.
- The highwayman said he would return later that night.
- He kissed her and rode away.

b The setting is dark and cloudy. This symbolises that the highwayman was in danger.
c He'd a French cocked-hat on his forehead, a bunch of lace at his chin, A coat of the claret velvet, and breeches of brown doe-skin.
d Tim is described in an unattractive way: his face was white and peaked; His eyes were hollows of madness, his hair like mouldy hay.
e Open question.
f He attracted her attention by whistling a tune – this must have been their pre-arranged signal.
g Although he may be harassed by soldiers trying to capture him, he will return later that night.
h Blood, passion
i Describing the ostler as being jealous, hinting that the highwayman is in danger.

Student's Book page 117
Speaking

Ask learners to predict how the ballad ends. Write the predictions on the board for future reference.

Weekly review

Level	Reading	Listening and speaking
■	Learner has not engaged sufficiently with the text.	Learner found it difficult to focus on and interpret the text being read to him. Learner made very little effort to create an interesting sports commentary.
●	Learner engaged satisfactorily with the text.	Learner listened attentively to the text being read aloud. Learner was able to interpret the text fairly accurately. Learner created a good sports commentary.
▲	Learner engaged extremely well with the text.	Learner listened attentively and was able to interpret the finer nuances of the text with mature insight. Learner created a highly entertaining sports commentary.

Week 3

Student's Book pages 117–123

Workbook pages 55–60

Student's Book pages 117–119

Listening

Instruct learners to listen to the second part of the poem.

Workbook pages 55–56

Reading and vocabulary

Answers
1

a French cocked-hat	an old-fashioned three corner hat
claret	dark red, like wine
pistol butts	the handles of the pistols
rapier	a long thin sword
stable-wicket	stable door
ostler	a person who looks after horses at an inn
peaked	having a sickly look
harry me	chase me
casement	window
tawny	yellow, golden
musket	an old-fashioned rifle
jest	joke, mock
priming	charging muskets with gunpowder
blanched	went pale

2
a blue
b helper
c rapier
d shutter
e busy
f pressure

3
Open question.

Student's Book page 119

Comprehension

Answers
a Tim, the jealous ostler, must have told them.
b A fair chance to be successful
c Open question.
d Own response
e Open question.
f By repeating the drumming sound of the horse's hooves and by engaging directly with the reader through asking questions.
g Breaking the narrative with short bursts of the horse's hooves. Repeating 'nearer' and describing Bess's actions in detail.
h Tension is further created by letting the reader know what is waiting for the Highwayman.
i Open question.
j Open question.
k Man vs man – the jealousy of Tim cost the Highwayman and Bess their lives. Own opinion.
l The Highwayman and Bess die.
m Tim, the ostler, would have to decide whether or not to report the Highwayman, Bess would have to make the choice to kill herself.
n The Highway man is killed.
o Open question.

p The two verses tell about how the highwayman and Bess's love have turned into a legend.

Student's Book pages 120–121
Reading and writing

1 Read through and explain the structure of the first verse.

Answers

2

a
- The wind was a torrent of darkness among the gusty trees – The wind is howling through the trees the way a river would rage during a flood.
- The moon was a ghostly galleon tossed upon cloudy seas – the moon appears to be moving as clouds cover its surface sporadically.
- The road was a ribbon of moonlight over the purple moor – the road twists and turns over the moor.

3

a The short syllables forces the reader to adopt a rhythm that reminds us of a horse galloping. It is a strong beat. This builds up tension.
b The reader is 'galloping' through the verse, and because the reader knows what has already happened, tension builds in anticipation of the highwayman's sure fate.

5

a The pace of the first verse is 'smooth' whilst the second is 'choppy'
b A choppy rhythm creates energy and drama.
c Tlot tlot, clattered, tapped
d There would be far less drama as the words flow too smoothly.

Workbook pages 57–58
Grammar

Answers

1

Figurative Language Technique.	What does this suggest/mean?
Metaphor The wind was a torrent of darkness among the gusty trees	This shows us that the wind was howling because the word 'torrent' means a rush, or deluge. The metaphor creates a sense of unease as it describes the wind as bringing a torrent of darkness which could be interpreted as a warning of bad news.
Metaphor The hours crawled by like years	She waited a long, long time.
Simile He spurred like a madman	He rode as fast as he could.
Alliteration Down like a dog in the highway	Strong emphasis of the 'd' sound adds emphasis and drama
Onomatopoeia Tlot tlot	This sounds like a horse's hooves

Differentiation
Extension

- Instruct learners to work with a partner, and copying the poem's structure, to write an alternative ending to the poem, where poor Bess doesn't die!
- Let learners log on to YouTube and listen to Fleetwood Mac's rendition of 'The Highwayman' called 'Everywhere'.
- Give learners an opportunity to do extra research on highwaymen.

Support

- Instruct learners to work with a partner, and to write an alternative ending to the poem, where poor Bess doesn't die!

Student's Book page 121

Grammar

Answers

1
a I'm frightened of the guards because they can hurt me.
b I have to free myself as I have to warn my love.
c I will never get free because the ropes are too tightly tied.
d I'm going to pull the trigger when I hear horse's hooves.

2
a I can't stand the way she smiles at him as it hurts me.
b I'm furious with that criminal because he does not deserve Bess.
c I'm going to tell the King's guards that he's returning tonight.
d I wish I had never betrayed the highwayman because now I have killed the woman I love.

Student's Book page 122

Vocabulary

Answers

1
a Likeable **b** Believable **c** Loveable
d Manageable **e** Excitable

2
a Happiness **b** Fear **c** Coward/cowardice
d Excitement **e** Peace

3
a Revolve **b** Simplify **c** Love
d Perform **e** pretend

Workbook pages 59–60

Grammar

Complete this summary of *The Highwayman* for homework.

Answers
1 Ballad, dramatic, doom, daughter, ostler, betray, soldiers, gag, escape, highwayman, sacrifice, ignorant, awful, inn, lovers
2 Open question.

Let learners work in pairs to write ten sentences about the poem. Use the word cloud vocabulary as a starting point, but encourage them to use their own ideas as well.

Student's Book page 123

Speaking

Divide learners into small groups. If possible, give each group a copy of the poem (but if not, it is in their Student's Book in two parts. Instruct learners to prepare their designated section/s of the ballad. Arrange the groups in the same sequence as the verses of the poem. Let them recite the poem. If possible, make a video recording of learners and play it back to them. Point out strengths and weaknesses and give the groups an opportunity to make any necessary adjustments to their performances. Rerecord and play back, showing the groups how they have improved.

Student's Book page 123

Writing

Revise the structure of a newspaper article. Write the points on the board. Instruct learners to write a report of the highwayman's death.

Weekly review

Level	Reading	Writing	Listening and speaking
■	Learner has a poor understanding of figurative language. Learner has shown very little understanding of the grammar in this unit.	Learner's news article was of a poor standard.	Learner made little effort in the group choral verse activity.
●	Learner has a good understanding of figurative language. Learner has shown satisfactory understanding of the grammar in this unit.	Learner wrote a satisfactory news article.	Learner contributed well in the group choral verse activity.
▲	Learner has a sound understanding of figurative language. Learner has shown an excellent understanding of the grammar in this unit.	Learner wrote an accurate news article.	Learner's contribution to the group choral verse activity ensured its success.

Formal assessment 3

To assess the main learning objectives in Units 7, 8 and 9, have learners do Formal assessment 1 independently. Mark the assessment and record relevant assessment information.

Mark scheme

Question 1
Learners can either read the poem silently, or they can take turns to read it aloud if you want to assess their ability to read aloud meaningfully.

A Autumn has arrived, and leaves have turned colour. The wind blows dead leaves off trees. Winter is on its way. (2)

B Simile: Autumn arrives/ Like an experienced robber (2)

C What do the following phrases in the poem refer to? (3)
- green leaves
- autumn leaves
- the gusts of wind

D grabbing the green stuff (1)

E The diversions are planned to make them effective, so that the wind can blow the leaves off the trees. (1)

F calm (1)

G literal: winter has arrived

figurative: winter has stolen warmth from the world. (2)

H Learner must justify his/her opinion (2)

Question 2
A (5)
- The wind **howled** relentlessly throughout the night.
- The rain **has been falling** for three hours!
- It **is** a cloudy day.
- I **love** the smell of the garden after the rain.
- It **seems** rather chilly today.

Question 3
A (4)

Example:
- Line 1: Little Miss Muffet sat on her tuffet (past perfect tense)
  Answer: Little Miss Muffet **had sat on her tuffet.**
- Line 2: Eating her curds and whey (present perfect tense)
  She has eaten her curds and whey
- Line 3: When down came a spider (simple present tense)
  When a spider comes down
- Line 4: Who sat down beside her (future continuous/progressive tense)
  The spider will be sitting down beside her.
- Line 5: And frightened Miss Muffet away. (simple present tense)
  It frightens Miss Muffet away.

Question 4
A (4)
- The old woman smells the beautiful roses. (action verb)
- The athlete's feet smell really bad! (linking verb)
- Some parents become quite emotional when their children go to school for the first time. (being verb)
- Global warming is affecting the weather. (being verb)

Question 5
A (6)

Abstract noun	Descriptive adjective	Adverb of manner	Verb
revolution	revolving		revolve
	likeable	likely	like
happiness	happy	happily	

Question 6
Mark learners on the following:
- Strong topic sentence (1 mark)
- Use of persuasive techniques (4 marks)
- Use of connectives between ideas and sentences (1 mark)
- Correct sentence structure, punctuation and spelling. (1 mark)

Stage 6   PCM 1

Summary activity

Chapter One	Chapter Two	Chapter Three
Topic sentence	Topic sentence	Topic sentence
Supporting facts	Supporting facts	Supporting facts
Supporting facts	Supporting facts	Supporting facts
Supporting facts	Supporting facts	Supporting facts

© HarperCollins*Publishers* Ltd. 2016

Debate worksheet

Motion (the topic)	
My first point	What you plan to say:
	Develop your point:
My second point	What you plan to say:
	Develop your point:
My third point	What you plan to say:
	Develop your point:

Conclusion: Remind the audience of what you have said. End on a strong note.

Stage 6

PCM 2 Page 2 of 2

My team's points to discuss	_____ Speaker's points	_____ Speaker's points
	1	1
	2	2
	3	3
Rebuttal	The other team said:	But we disagree because…

© HarperCollins*Publishers* Ltd. 2016

Stage 6 PCM 3

San Columbo Times

Stage 6 PCM 4

Role play checklist and assessment criteria

Checklist for role play	
Does your role play have a story line?	
Is your story line believable?	
Do your facial expressions and body language match your words?	
Do both characters have a similar amount of dialogue?	
Have you practised your lines?	
Will your audience hear you clearly?	
Is your character believable?	

Peer assessment

Assessment criteria	✔	✘
The plot is sensible and easy to understand		
The characters are well portrayed		
The dialogue flows smoothly		
I could hear the dialogue clearly		
The dialogue is very funny		

© HarperCollins*Publishers* Ltd. 2016

Character description

Character	Information about the character	Proof from the text
Spud	Is nervous about going to boarding school.	'…my heart is beating like a bongo drum'
Mr Milton		
Mrs Milton		

Stage 6

The possessive apostrophe

1 Change the phrase in the first column into a phrase using an apostrophe in the second column.

the lead belonging to the dog	*the dog's lead*
the sweet belonging to Ann	
the friend of John	
the house of the brothers	
the cat belonging to Paulina	
the campus of the college	
the toys belonging to the children	
the sister of the twins	
the adventure of the women	

2 Read the following sentences, paying careful attention to the underlined words. If the underlined word is correctly punctuated, circle 'Yes'. If the underlined word is incorrectly punctuated, circle 'No', and write the correction on the line provided.

a The pop stars dressing room was decorated with cream furniture because she insisted on having a room with a peaceful mood.

Yes   No   _____

b The dressing room had to be draped in cream or soft pink. It couldn't be dark.

Yes   No   _____

c There were three coffee tables' in the room.

Yes   No   _____

d The fans' screams were deafening!

Yes   No   _____

e The mens' behaviour at the concert was embarrassing.

Yes   No   _____

Collective nouns

A Nuisance of Nouns

An abandonment of orphans
A ballet dance of swans
A crush of rhinoceroses
A dose of doctors
An elephant of enormities
A fidget of school children
A glacier of fridges
A hover of hawks
An inquisition of judges
A Jonah of shipwrecks
A knuckle of robbers
A lottery of dice
A misery of bullets
A number of mathematicians
An outrage of stars
A prayer of nuns
A quake of cowards
A roundabout of arguments
A swelter of duvets
A tangle of tricksters
An upset of horoscopes
A vein of goldfinch
A wonder of stars
An x-ray of soothsayers
A zeal of enthusiasts.

Stage 6

Contractions

1 **Complete the following sentences so that they make sense. Choose the missing words from the box below. The words may be used more than once.**

> your   you're   its   it's   his   she's

1 The bird stretched _____ wings.

2 _____ going to play football this afternoon.

3 _____ a beautiful day.

4 Adam is looking for _____ pen.

5 My friend found _____ book on the floor.

6 _____ responsible for your own property.

7 My neighbour says _____ going to paint her house.

8 _____ interesting to watch a lion catch _____ prey.

2 **Write your own sentences. Use each word from the box below in one of your sentences. Underline the contraction.**

> couldn't   won't   can't   isn't   shan't   wasn't   mustn't

_____

_____

_____

_____

_____

_____

_____

Comparison table

Similarities	David Copperfield	Malala's Blog	The hole in the wall project
Content			
Point of view			

Differences	David Copperfield	Malala's Blog	The hole in the wall project
Vocab			
Text characteristics			
Content			

Stage 6

PCM 10

Sentences with adjectives

Make your own sentences by filling in the table. Remember that a proper adjective begins with a capital letter. Write your sentences on the lines underneath the table.

possessive adjective	descriptive adjective	common noun	verb	proper adjective
My	beautiful	friend	is	German

_____

_____

_____

_____

_____

_____

_____

© HarperCollins*Publishers* Ltd. 2016

Stage 6

Sentence work

1 **Rearrange the words so that they make meaningful sentences.**

   a book have a you read good lately? _____

   b days seven are there week a in. _____

   c must exciting travel be time! _____

   d to to make our decisions need all we be make able own.
   _____

   e of is a story ideas journey a. _____

   f world Jonas' there no is pain war or in.
   _____

   g choose to would live such in you world a?
   _____

   h allocated new children to units family are.
   _____

   i he saw different because Jonas colour flashes was of.
   _____

   j same the was everyone. _____

2 **Underline the predicate in the following sentences:**

   a Jonas and his friends rode bicycles.
   b The children sat on chairs.
   c The family units ate their meals at the same time.
   d Do you play sport at school?992
   e Can you choose your own career?

> Change questions into statements to find the subject and predicate.

3 **Fill in the missing subjects**

   a _____ is my cousin.

   b _____ and I plan to watch a movie tonight.

   c _____ is my favourite food.

   d _____ is the capital of my country.

   e _____ are dangerous animals.

Structure of a story

Plot	Structure	Planning
1 Introduction	introduce the setting and main character/s	
2 Rising action	events leading up to the climax/drama	
3 Climax	the drama caused by the problem	
4 Falling action	what happens after the drama	
5 Resolution	ending off the story	

Stage 6

Spelling

**Draw lines from the word to the sentence that is missing the word.
Use different pen shades to make the lines clearer to follow.**

compulsion	I'd like to hear your _____ of events.
convulsion	They had to drive around the _____.
emulsion	Rocket _____ has enabled space travel.
expulsion	She had a _____ to help others.
propulsion	The class went out on an _____.
version	The naughty boy was threatened with _____.
conversion	The _____ from Dollars to Yen was difficult to make.
diversion	The room was painted in white _____ paint.
excursion	The joke was met with _____.

© HarperCollins*Publishers* Ltd. 2016

Stage 6

Summary table

Animal	Habitat	Eating habits	Appearance	Hunting method	Interesting facts
Praying Mantis					
Tarantula					
Scorpion					
Weta					
Mossy Frog					

The structure of a sentence

A simple sentence contains only a single clause, while a compound sentence, a complex sentence, or a compound-complex sentence contains at least two clauses.

The simple sentence

The most basic type of sentence is the **simple sentence** which contains only one clause. A simple sentence can be as short as one word, such as "Run!"

Usually, however, the sentence has a subject as well as a predicate. All of the following are simple sentences, because each contains only one clause:

- **Run**!
- Run quickly!
- The boy runs quickly.
- The boy in the park **runs** quickly to the swings.
- Dressed warmly, the boy in the park **runs** quickly to the swings.

As you can see, a simple sentence can be quite long – it is a mistake to think that you can tell a simple sentence from a compound sentence or a complex sentence simply by its length.

The compound sentence

A **compound sentence** consists of two or more main clauses (or simple sentences) joined by co-ordinating conjunctions like 'and', 'but' and 'or'. The co-ordinating conjunctions can be remembered with the acronym FANBOYS which stands for: for, and, nor, but, or, yet, so.

A compound sentence is most effective when you use it to create a sense of balance or contrast between two (or more) equally-important pieces of information.

Simple: I love chocolate cake.
Simple: I bake every week.
Compound: I love chocolate cake, so I bake every week.

© HarperCollins*Publishers* Ltd. 2016

Stage 6

1 Combine the pairs of sentences with the connective in brackets.

   a The wind was howling. I was freezing. (and)

   b It was raining. It didn't matter! (but)

   c The bird flew away. It got a fright. (for)

   d I may watch TV. I may play outside. (or)

   e It's sunny outside. I'm going to swim! (so)

2 A sentence must contain a complete idea.
Decide whether or not each of the sentences below is complete or incomplete.
Write 'I' for incomplete, or 'C' for complete in the blanks provided.

   a _____ The tiny squirrel running along the fence.

   b _____ The chipmunk was climbing the tree.

   c _____ My pet turtle has four legs.

   d _____ The baseball bat.

   e _____ My older sister.

   f _____ My best friend is coming over this weekend.

   g _____ The strangest thing I've ever seen

Stage 6

PCM 16

More about sentences

1 Using the picture as inspiration, write a simple sentence, a compound sentence and a complex sentence. Write your sentences below each of the examples.

a **Simple sentence:** The teacher is reading a book.

b **Compound sentence:** The teacher is reading a book and the children are listening.

c **Complex sentence:** The teacher is reading a book to the class because they love listening to stories.

2 Expand your simple sentence into a sentence of 20 syllables.

Example:

Simple sentence: The teacher is reading a book

20 syllables: The teacher reads a wonderful book about dragons to his diligent students.

© HarperCollins*Publishers* Ltd. 2016

Group evaluation

Stage 6 — PCM 17

Pretend you and your team are representatives of the government who have to decide which proposal to choose for the Juvenile Detention Centre. Study the criteria carefully and award appropriate scores for each presentation you watch.

Content	The group has provided all the required information: • Name of the centre • How many offenders will be housed there? • Will you accept all offenders, or only those who have committed specific crimes? Why? • What tasks would the offenders carry out, if any? • What relaxation facilities would be provided for the offenders? How will this help improve behaviour? • What education would be provided for the offenders? Why? • Describe a typical day at the centre. • Who would work at the centre? What sort of personalities would they have? • What sort of security would you have at the centre? • How would the offenders be motivated to change their behaviour?	0–20
Flow of information	The presentation flowed smoothly and logically.	0–5
Visuals	A plan/photo/drawing was displayed to add value to the presentation. The visual was appropriate and of an excellent quality.	0–5
Presentation	Well-rehearsed, with each member contributing. Interesting and convincing introduction and conclusion.	0–10
Questions and answer session	Group was able to answer all the questions adequately and sensibly.	0–5
Total mark		

© HarperCollins*Publishers* Ltd. 2016

Stage 6 PCM 18

Connectives

**❶ Read the text carefully. Fill in the missing connectives.
Choose words from the box to complete the sentences sensibly.**

> begin   finally   when   after   first   then

Write the words in the spaces. Some words may be used twice.

> ### Where do black holes come from?
>
> Black holes are formed from some kinds of stars _____ they get old and die. Not all stars turn into black holes, only the biggest ones. Stars don't last forever. _____ burning for billions of years, they get old and _____ to run out of fuel. It still takes a long time for a star to die – it can be millions of years. _____, the star swells up and turns red. Most stars _____ shrink and cool down into a small, heavy ball of ash – a dead star. These dead stars are about the size of Earth, but much heavier – as heavy as the Sun.
>
> _____ a really giant star starts to die, it doesn't just get bigger, it explodes. The star _____ collapses in on itself and shrinks to a tiny size. It becomes much smaller than a normal dead star. _____, it becomes so tiny, it's just a very, very heavy dot in space. This is a black hole.

❷ Write your own sentences. Use a connective from the box in each sentence.

> as   soon   as   now   that   since   while   until

_____

_____

_____

_____

© HarperCollins*Publishers* Ltd. 2016

Persuasive essay A

Identify the different persuasive strategies the writer has used in this essay about children watching too much television.

- Colour code the boxes around the text in different colours.
- Match the boxes to their examples in the essay.
- Colour code the bolded sentences to match the boxes.

| Refer to an expert's opinion |
| Rhetorical questions |
| Alliteration |
| Three items in a row |
| Statistics |
| Speaking directly to the reader |
| Emotive language |
| Contrasting language |

If there's one thing I hate, it's seeing children sitting mindlessly in front of a television! Seriously, who in their right mind can approve of young minds being **numbed by canned laughter, ridiculous plots and cheesy characters**? I think television is the worst thing ever invented – it's a legal mind-drug!

According to Jane Healy, PhD, author of *Endangered Minds: Why Children Don't Think – and What We Can Do About It,* children who watch too much TV struggle to use their own ideas to create something out of nothing. Sadly, when children play make-believe, the play tends to be based on their favourite shows. **Is this what we want?** Is this fair to young minds? **Surely we are letting them down** by deliberately blocking their young minds from developing creatively? What kind of future is waiting for these **TV test tubes**?

Another problem caused by children watching television, is that they begin to believe that all life's problems can be solved (often through crime and immoral behaviour!) and that needs and wants will be met immediately. You how it is – the soap opera characters who die and then suddenly appear alive and well on the show – no questions asked. Ridiculous! Or what about characters who commit the most hurtful deeds with no consequences? That's right – **TV teaches tiny tots** that it's fine to lie and cheat and steal … no-one gets punished on the box, so why should they? **Small wonder these young children are so confused!**

TV is addictive. **The average American child watches three hours a day of TV.** Three hours! The child could rather be playing sport, riding a bike or learning a craft. Or what about flying a kite, building a treehouse or interacting with family members? How can children learn socially-appropriate communication skills when they're only engaging with the flickering of a screen. It's so, so sad. **I'm not saying that children should never watch TV, but I do say that viewing time should be limited.**

The final point I wish to discuss is how TV stunts language development. Children are so used to having people speak for them – they are mere bystanders, watching strangers become closer than family, so what need do they have of developing a vocabulary? Why do they need to listen closely? Why do they need to think actively? They don't – the box that rules the family, rules them! And destroys them!

So, do you want to disempower children by blocking their creativity and stunting their communication skills? I should think not! We need to actively encourage the guardians of our future to be free-thinkers and problem-solvers. Get rid of television! **You can do it!**

Stage 6   PCM 20

Persuasive essay B

Identify the different persuasive strategies the writer has used in this essay about children watching too much television.

- Colour code the boxes around the text in different colours.
- Match the boxes to their examples in the essay.
- Colour code the sentences to match the boxes.

| Refer to an expert's opinion |

| Rhetorical questions |

| Alliteration |

| Three items in a row |

| Statistics |

| Speaking directly to the reader |

| Emotive language |

| Contrasting pairs |

If there's one thing I hate, it's seeing children sitting mindlessly in front of a television! Seriously, who in their right mind can approve of young minds being numbed by canned laughter, ridiculous plots and cheesy characters? I think television is the worst thing ever invented – it's a legal mind-drug!

According to Jane Healy, PhD, author of *Endangered Minds: Why Children Don't Think – and What We Can Do About It,* children who watch too much TV struggle to use their own ideas to create something out of nothing. Sadly, when children play make-believe, the play tends to be based on their favourite shows. Is this what we want? Is this fair to young minds? Surely we are letting them down by deliberating blocking their young minds from developing creatively? What kind of future is waiting for these TV test tubes?

Another problem caused by children watching television, is that they begin to believe that all life's problems can be solved (often through crime and immoral behaviour!) and that needs and wants will be met immediately. You how it is – the soap opera characters who die and then suddenly appear alive and well on the show – no questions asked. Ridiculous! Or what about characters who commit the most hurtful deeds with no consequences? That's right – TV teaches tiny tots that it's fine to lie and cheat and steal … no-one gets punished on the box, so why should they? Small wonder these young children are so confused!

TV is addictive. The average American child watches three hours a day of TV. Three hours! The child could rather be playing sport, riding a bike or learning a craft. Or what about flying a kite, building a treehouse or interacting with family members? How can children learn socially-appropriate communication skills when they're only engaging with the flickering of a screen. It's so, so sad. I'm not saying that children should never watch TV, but I do say that viewing time should be limited.

The final point I wish to discuss is how TV stunts language development. Children are so used to having people speak for them – they are mere bystanders, watching strangers become closer than family, so what need do they have of developing a vocabulary? Why do they need to listen closely? Why do they need to think actively? They don't – the box that rules the family, rules them! And destroys them!

So, do you want to disempower children by blocking their creativity and stunting their communication skills? I should think not! We need to actively encourage the guardians of our future to be free-thinkers and problem-solvers. Get rid of television! You can do it!

© HarperCollins*Publishers* Ltd. 2016

A balanced argument

"It is about time we brought back corporal punishment."
Do you agree with this view?

Corporal/capital punishment is _____

_____

_____

_____

There are a number of reasons why _____

_____

Firstly _____

_____

_____

_____

Secondly _____

_____

_____

_____

However _____

_____

_____

_____

I agree with _____

because _____

_____

_____

_____

Verbs – present tense

1 Present Tense – simple or progressive? Fill in the correct form.

a You can't see Ben now. He _____ a rest. (have)

b He usually _____ milk, but today he _____ water. (drink, drink)

c I won't go out now because it _____ and I _____ an umbrella. (rain, not have)

d Nowadays, women usually _____ hats. (not wear)

e Who _____ that terrible noise? It is Sameer.
He _____ his nose. (make, blow)

f My mother always keeps _____ me to brush my teeth. (tell)

g My neighbour seldom _____ to the theatre. (go)

h I _____ this weekend with my grandmother. I _____ her nearly every week. (spend, visit)

i My sister always keeps _____ for more pocket money. (ask)

j Who _____ to on the phone? (you speak)

2 Fill in the correct form of the perfect tense.

a The building _____ here for many years. (be)

b We _____ chess for the last few hours. (play)

c We _____ problems with our new computer recently. (have)

d _____ anything interesting lately? (you see)

e South Africa _____ a democracy since 1994. (be)

f I _____ care of my neighbour's cats while they are away. (take)

g I _____ my bike for three years. (have)

h John and Mary _____ all morning. (irritate)

i It _____ hard since last night (rain).

j I'm tired because I _____ well lately. (not feel)

3 Circle the correct answer:

a Look! Tracey is bringing / brings her little sister to class.

b My cousin is often listening / often listens to pop music.

c We are writing / write a test now.

d Hooray! Aurelia is baking / bakes a cake.

e Our teacher is giving / gives us a test every month.

f Listen! Mrs Choudhry is reading / reads a story to her class.

g Mr Prag usually is growing / grows roses in his garden.

h They are building / build a new school.

i Rishi is drinking / drinks milk every morning.

j Look! The boy is running / runs down the hill.

Verbs – past tense

Stage 6
PCM 23 • Sheet 1 of 2

1 **Complete these sentences in the PAST TENSE, using the correct verb.**

> play   enjoy   watch   listen   talk   phone   watch
> stop   walk   travel   like   stay

a We really _____ the concert last week. It was great!

b She _____ with friends in France last summer.

c Italy _____ very well in the match last night.

d Her parents _____ by plane from London to Germany.

e I _____ you three times last night but you were out.

f We _____ along the beach yesterday. It was lovely.

g She _____ the main course but she didn't like the dessert.

h The men _____ work at exactly one o'clock.

i _____ to the new One Direction song yesterday. It's great.

j I _____ the late film on TV last night.

2 **Fill in the blanks with a correct form of PAST CONTINUOUS.**

a Noor hurt herself while she _____ (skate).

b I met my neighbour while I _____ (walk) home from town.

c Sally saw a friend while she _____ (ride) her bicycle from school.

d Peter fell asleep while he _____ (study).

e Bob stepped on my feet while we _____ (dance) together.

f I cut myself while I _____ (peel) potatoes.

g Tom and Jerry burned themselves while they _____ (bake).

h Tommy had a nightmare while he _____ (sleep) at a friend's house.

© HarperCollins*Publishers* Ltd. 2016

Stage 6

3 What's the matter?

	What was he / she doing?	What happened?	What's the result?
Gary	play football	kick the goalpost	break leg
Sarah	ice-skate	fall on the ice	break foot
Lily	dance	trip over the carpet	sprain ankle
Mpho	cycle	fall off the bike	injure hand
Jonas	run	bump into a pole	Hurt head

Make dialogues as in the example:

You : Hi, Sarah! What's the matter with your foot?
Tina: I broke it.
You: How did it happen?
Tina: I fell on the ice while I was ice-skating.

You: _____

Gary: _____

You: _____

Gary: _____

You: _____

Sarah: _____

You: _____

Sarah: _____

You: _____

Lily: _____

You: _____

Lily: _____

You: _____

Mpho: _____

You: _____

Mpho: _____

You: _____

Jonas: _____

You: _____

Jonas: _____

© HarperCollins*Publishers* Ltd. 2016

Verbs – future tense
Future continuous

1 Make sentences with 'will be –*ing*.

  a I'm going to watch television from 6pm until 8pm this evening.
     So at 5.55pm I _____
     _____

  b Tomorrow afternoon I'm going to play tennis from 3 pm until 4.30pm.
     So at 2pm tomorrow I _____
     _____

  c Jim is going to study from 4.30 pm until 8pm this evening.
     So at 8.30 this evening he _____
     _____

  d I am going to clean my room tomorrow. It will take from 9am until 11am.
     So at 10 am tomorrow morning _____
     _____

2 Make sentences with the future perfect tense.

  a By next March, I _____ (write) my third book.

  b I hope you _____ (not / forget) your spelling words by tomorrow.

  c By next week we _____ (redecorate) the house.

  d Next month she _____ (be) in Australia for two years.

  e I hope I will _____ (not / make) a lot of mistakes in the exam.

Stage 6

3 Join each idea in A with an idea from B. Make sentences using 'was' / 'were going to' and the verbs in brackets.

A
I (take) a taxi home last night,
I (drive) to town,
We (play) tennis,
Dan (eat) the cake,
They (watch) a movie,

B
but then it stated to rain, so we played scrabble instead.
but my friend offered me a lift instead.
but they decided to go for a walk instead.
but he decided on an apple instead.
but I decided to take the bus instead.

_____

_____

_____

_____

_____

4 Fill in the blanks with the correct future forms.

a "What _____ you _____ (do) when you grow up?"

"I _____ (be) an acrobat in a circus."

b I haven't seen my cousin for a long time but I'm sure I _____ (recognise) him.

c "I need some money to buy a shirt."

"I _____ (give) you some."

d I got the plane tickets. I _____ (fly) on Tuesday.

e "Have you got any plans for the summer?"

"Yes, we _____ (go) to India in June."

Prepared oral planning sheet

Introduction	Explain why you are talking
Connect to first paragraph	Write a connecting sentence.
Paragraph one	General autobiographical background
Connect to second paragraph	Write a connecting sentence.
Paragraph two	Training to be a spy
Connect to third paragraph	Write a connecting sentence.
Paragraph three	Duties and responsibilities of a spy
Conclusion	Recap End off

© HarperCollins*Publishers* Ltd. 2016

Stage 6

PCM 26

Unstressed vowels

**Study the list of words.
Rewrite the words on the lines that have been drawn.
Colour code the unstressed vowels in each word.**

difference

deafening

generous

interested

general

miserable

different

jewellery

offering

secretary

dictionary

primary

literacy

boundary

stationary

voluntary

library

© HarperCollins*Publishers* Ltd. 2016

Formal assessment 1 (Units 1–3)

Question 1

Reading

Read the following extract from *Alone at Sea* by Liam O Flynn
Answer the questions in full sentences.

> Water, water, everywhere and not a drop to drink. I am doomed. The wooden planks of **flotsam** I **cobbled** together after the shipwreck are coming loose. I am sitting on a floating coffin with makeshift oars. It's like a sauna out here in this big, blue tomb. The emptiness in my soul matches the **spiritless** sky and the featureless waterscape around me.
>
> The days are the worst. The **remorseless** sun bends his full will against my survival and he is winning. I feel like I have been stabbed by a million sun spears. My blood simmers, my brain stews, and even my bones seem to smoulder in their meaty carcass. Dead man drifting. That's who I am. I am **floundering** in a sea of divine-blue quicklime and there's no escape. My tongue feels like a slab of lead, **cloven** to the roof of my mouth. My throat is parched and my lips are chapped and flaky. Below the surface, huge shapes glide. Their fins break the surface like steel triangles, leaving barely a ripple. They circle and circle, constantly searching for weakness. They have followed me for three days and nights, cruel and cunning as they are. The knife fixed to the end of the oar can only keep them at bay for so long.
>
> The haunting cheep-cheep of a passing tern reminds me how powerless I really am. Even he can go home. The stink of a thousand seas surrounds me. It is a mix of rotting kelp and dying fish. It assaults my nostrils and steals my hope.
>
> But lo! There's a huge magma-red light in the distance. I am rocked by a huge wave which pushes me towards the light. My name is Lucius Andropedus. I am a fisherman from Pompeii and I am lost at sea.

A Give synonyms for the bold words in the extract. (5)

flotsam _____

cobbled _____

spiritless _____

floundering _____

cloven _____

Stage 6 — Formal assessment 1

B Why does the fisherman say that he is sitting on a floating coffin? (2)

C To what is the sea being compared in the first paragraph? (1)

D Quote, and explain, a simile from the first paragraph. (2)

E Why is the seascape described as being featureless? (1)

F Why is there no escape for the fisherman from the divine blue quicklime? (2)

G Quote an example of alliteration in the text. (1)

H The 'huge magma-red light in the distance' is a volcanic eruption. Do you think he has been saved? (2)

I From whose perspective is this extract written? Quote from the text to support your answer. (2)

J From which point of view is this extract written? (1)

K How can we tell that this extract is set hundreds of years ago? (1)

© HarperCollins*Publishers* Ltd. 2016

Stage 6 Formal assessment 1

Question 2

Grammar

A Name the parts of speech of the underlined words in the text extract below. Fill your answers in the table below the extract. (4)

> Water, <u>water</u>, everywhere and not a drop to drink. I am <u>doomed</u>. The <u>wooden</u> planks of flotsam I cobbled together after the shipwreck are coming loose. I am sitting on a floating coffin with makeshift oars. It's like a sauna out here in this big, blue tomb. The <u>emptiness</u> in my soul matches the spiritless sky and the featureless waterscape around me.

Word from text	Part of speech
water	
doomed	
wooden	
emptiness	

B Identify the parts of speech of the underlined words in the following sentences. Only write down the answer. (4)

- The tern cheeped <u>hauntingly</u>. _____

- The sailor was a fisherman from <u>Pompeii</u>. _____

- A huge wave pushed the raft towards the <u>Italian</u> coast. _____

- The adventure happened <u>many years ago</u>. _____

C Rewrite the following sentences, punctuating them correctly. (4)

- It is important to check your boat before going out to sea

_____

- The fishermans adventure was dangerous!

_____

- Have you ever had a lucky escape

_____

- Always pack extra food warm clothing and a flare.

_____

© HarperCollins*Publishers* Ltd. 2016

Stage 6   **Formal assessment 1**

D Study the picture below to help you answer the questions that follow. (4)

- Write a sentence about the picture in active voice.

  _____

- Write a sentence about the picture in passive voice.

  _____

- Write an opinion about the picture.

  _____

- Write a fact about the picture.

  _____

E Change the words below into nouns. (4)

- describe   _____
- confident   _____
- fragrant   _____
- musical   _____

© HarperCollins*Publishers* Ltd. 2016

Stage 6   Formal assessment 2

Formal assessment 2 (Units 4–6)
Question 1

Read the following text carefully:

Tarantula: another name for terror

by Terri Coffman (http://www.belizeans.com/taran.html)

Catchy title, huh? However, it's not exactly accurate. To be more precise, at least as far as I'm concerned, terror is ANY spider. Size is not relative. The clinical term for my fear is arachnophobia — the fear of spiders — and mine was born one rainy night in the middle of a Central American Rainforest when I was eleven years old. It has had a profound effect on my life ever since.

Living in the jungle in Belize, in a thatched roof house with open doors and windows, one became accustomed to all kinds of unwelcome visitors. But the most unwelcome of all was a big, black, hairy tarantula that stretched close to 25 cm from leg to leg and stood almost 12 cm high. Unfortunately for him as well as for me, he fell from the wall into my bed, covering the entire indentation on the pillow where my face would have been. In the split seconds that followed my ear-splitting screams, the monstrous thing was killed by my broom-wielding dad. And, as Fate would have it, the spider ended up in my bed a second time, this time squashed and mangled, and definitely dead.

I remember just standing there, numb, watching my dad toss the mangled mess out the window. Then, somewhere from a hazy distance, I heard my mom say the bedding was changed and it was alright to go back to bed, but I was paralyzed. I couldn't move. I was literally frozen with fear! Only one thought kept flashing through my mind: what if that spider had fallen on my face while I was sleeping? What if.....? What if.....? What if.....?

Logically, I knew the poor thing was just as frightened as I was. It wasn't lying in wait to attack me; it was simply trying get out of the rain, and if I had not knocked it off the wall getting into bed, the tarantula would have, in all probability, gone up into the eaves of the roof to find food, and we would have never known it was up there. To this day, rationally, I know spiders, in general, are beneficial to man, but the mere mention of the word sends chills through me.

© HarperCollins*Publishers* Ltd. 2016

Stage 6   **Formal assessment 2**

Answer the following questions carefully, in full sentences. Remember to keep your answers in context at all times.

A Why is the title catchy? (1)

B What is the suffix for 'fear of'? (1)

C What is the difference between a rational fear and one that is irrational? (2)

D Pretend you are the girl who has just been frightened by the spider. You keep a diary. Write ONE sentence in your diary about the experience. (2)

E Pretend you are the girl's unsympathetic younger brother. You also keep a diary. Write ONE sentence about her experience. (2)

F Is this an informative text? Why/why not? (1)

G List three characteristics of an informative text. (3)

Question 2

A Read the paragraphs below carefully. Decide whether they have been correctly structured. Place a tick in the appropriate box below the paragraphs to reflect your assessment of the texts. (3)

Paragraph 1

Stanley Yelnats and his family have a history of bad luck. The first Stanley's great grandfather made a fortune on the stock market. The family's bad luck struck him when he moved from New York to California and was robbed by Kissin' Kate Barlow. Stanley's father is an inventor. He works very hard and is smart, however, none of his inventions ever work. Stanley is accused of a crime he didn't commit and is sent to Camp Green Lake as punishment. It seems none of the Yelnats can escape the family curse.

Paragraph 2

Camp Green Lake dried up and the people who lived near it moved away over a hundred years ago. Now the lake is desert-like with temperatures around ninety-five degrees. Deserts cover one-fifth of the Earth's surface. The only place to find shade is between two trees in the Warden's yard. Rattlesnakes and scorpions hide under rocks and in the holes the campers dig. Deserts do not have many large animals because there is not enough water for them to survive.

Paragraph 3

Stanley's father was an inventor. He was trying to discover a way to recycle old sneakers. Clatonia Joaquin Dorticus invented an apparatus for applying dyes to the sides of the soles and heels of shoes. George de Mestral invented Velcro. While hiking, he had noticed that burrs stuck to his clothing. He used this idea to develop one strip of nylon with loops, and another with hooks.

	Correctly structured	Incorrectly structured
Paragraph 1		
Paragraph 2		
Paragraph 3		

Stage 6 Formal assessment 2

Question 3

A **Name the underlined words in the following sentences below. (4)**

- The spider <u>was spinning a web</u>. _____

- <u>The spider</u> looks fierce. _____

- The spider was <u>in the garden</u>. _____

- The spider spins <u>beautifully</u>. _____

Question 4

A **Use the picture of the dinosaur to help you create interesting sentences. Follow the prompts for each sentence. (4)**

- End with an adverbial phrase of place.

  _____

  _____

- Include an adverb modifying a verb.

  _____

  _____

- Include an adverb modifying an adjective.

  _____

  _____

- Include an adverb modifying another adverb.

  _____

  _____

Stage 6   **Formal assessment 2**

Question 5

"I don't know why people are so scared of me."

A Rewrite Sally Spider's sentence in direct speech. Show that you know how to use the introductory verb in three different ways. (6)

Question 6

A Join the following pairs of sentences with a connective. Choose the most suitable connective from the box below. You may only use a connective once. Not all the connectives will be used. Check your punctuation carefully. (5)

> and   because   therefore   however   although   but   so

- The house in Belize had a thatched roof with open doors and windows. It is extremely hot in a jungle. (Because)

- Living in a jungle, one becomes used to all kinds of unwelcome visitors. The tarantula has to be the worst! (however)

- Henry doesn't mind spiders. They look scary. (although)

- The spider fell onto her bed. She screamed in panic. (and)

- We live in a jungle. We're used to all kinds of unwelcome visitors. (so)

© HarperCollins*Publishers* Ltd. 2016

Stage 6

Formal assessment 2

Question 7

A Underline the main clauses and circle the subordinate clauses in the following sentences. (5)

- Praying mantises, staying very still, wait for their prey to pass by.
- The mossy frog is hard to spot because it looks just like a piece of moss.
- Never pick up a scorpion, for its sting could make you very ill.
- Wetas, living in New Zealand, are one of the world's largest insects.
- As they can live till they're 30 years old, tarantulas are spider superstars.

Question 8

A Correct the punctuation of the following sentence in three different ways. You may not change or remove any of the words. (3)

The boy rushed home from school, he wanted to ride his new bike.

Formal assessment 3 (Units 7–9)

Question 1

Read the following poem carefully before answering the questions.

Autumn
by Alan Bold

Autumn arrives
Like an experienced robber
Grabbing the green stuff
Then cunningly covering his tracks
With a deep multitude
Of colourful distractions.
And the wind,
The wind is his accomplice
Putting an air of chaos
Into the careful diversions
So branches shake
And dead leaves are suddenly brown
In the faces of inquisitive strangers.
The theft chills the world
Changes the temper of the earth
Till the normally placid sky
Glows red with a quiet rage.

A In no more than twenty words, summarise this poem. (2)

B What figurative device does the poet use to describe autumn? Use a quote from the poem to substantiate your answer. (2)

Stage 6 Formal assessment 3

C What do the following phrases in the poem refer to? (3)
- 'the green stuff'

- 'colourful distractions'

- 'an air of chaos'

D Quote an example of alliteration. (1)

E Why are the diversions careful? (1)

F Give a synonym for 'placid'. (1)

G Give the literal and figurative interpretations/meanings for 'The theft chills the world'. (2)

H Which of the above interpretations is more accurate, in the context of the entire poem? Justify your answer carefully. (2)

Question 2

A Underline the verbs in the following sentences. (5)
- The wind howled relentlessly throughout the night.
- The rain has been falling for three hours!
- It is a cloudy day.
- I love the smell of the garden after the rain.
- It seems rather chilly today.

Stage 6

Formal assessment 3

Question 3

A Rewrite the lines of the nursery rhyme in different tenses.
You may have to add in some extra words.
Begin your answers with the given words. (4)

Example:

- Line 1: Little Miss Muffet sat on her tuffet (past perfect tense)
  Answer: Little Miss Muffet **had sat on her tuffet**.

- Line 2: Eating her curds and whey (present perfect tense)

  She _____

- Line 3: When down came a spider (simple present tense)

  When _____

- Line 4: Who sat down beside her (future continuous/progressive tense)

  The spider _____

- Line 5: And frightened Miss Muffet away. (simple present tense)

  It _____

Question 4

A Identify the type of verb in each sentence.
Write your answer on the line next to the sentence. (4)

- The old woman smells the beautiful roses. _____
- The athlete's feet smell really bad! _____
- Some parents become quite emotional when their children go to school for the first time. _____
- Global warming is affecting the weather. _____

Question 5

A Complete the table below. Change the words into different classes as specified. (6)

Abstract noun	Descriptive adjective	Adverb of manner	Verb
			revolve
		likely	
	happy		

Question 6

A Write a persuasive paragraph on one of the following topics. You may argue the topic from any perspective. (7)

- School uniforms should be compulsory.
- Global warming is serious!
- Refugees are problems.

_____
_____
_____
_____
_____
_____

Notes

© HarperCollins*Publishers* Ltd. 2016

Notes

© HarperCollins*Publishers* Ltd. 2016

Notes

Text acknowledgements
The publishers gratefully acknowledge the permissions granted to reproduce copyright material in the book. Every effort has been made to contact the holders of copyright material, but if any have been inadvertently overlooked, the Publisher will be pleased to make the necessary arrangements at the first opportunity.

HarperCollins*Publishers* Limited for an extract and artwork from *Hall of the Bulls* by Tom Bradman, illustrated by Nicholas Jackson, text copyright © Tom Bradman. Text reproduced by permission of HarperCollins*Publishers* Limited; David Higham Associates. HarperCollins*Publishers* Limited for an extract and artwork from *The Tear Jar* by Celia Rees, illustrated by Giorgio Bacchin, text copyright © Celia Rees. Text reproduced by permission of HarperCollins*Publishers* Limited; Sayle Literary Agency. HarperCollins*Publishers* Limited for an extract and artwork from *The Golden Turtle and other tales* by Gervase Phinn, illustrated by Tomislav Zlatic. Text reproduced by permission of HarperCollins*Publishers* and MBA Literary and Script Agency; artwork reproduced by permission of HarperCollins*Publishers* and Sylvie Poggo Artists. HarperCollins*Publishers* Limited for an extract and artwork from *What happened to the dinosaurs?*, written and illustrated by Jon Hughes, text. Text reproduced by kind permission of the author. HarperCollins*Publishers* Limited for an extract and artwork from *Weird Monsters*, written and illustrated by Nic Bishop, text copyright © Nic Bishop; for an extract and artwork from *Black Holes* by Anna Claybourne, illustrated by Steve Evans, text copyright © Anna Claybourne. Reproduced by kind permission of the author. HarperCollins*Publishers* Limited for an extract and artwork from *The Leopard Poachers* by Kathy Hoopmann, illustrated by Donna Acheson-Juillet, text copyright © Kathy Hoopmann; for an extract from *Virginia Hall: World War II Spy* by Adrian Bradbury, text copyright © Adrian Bradbury. Reproduced by kind permission of the author. HarperCollins*Publishers* Limited for an extract from *Becoming an Olympic Gymnast* by Beth Tweddle.

An extract from *Spud* by John van de Ruit, Penguin, 2005, pp.2-3, copyright © John van de Ruit, 2005, 2007. Reproduced by permission of Penguin Books Ltd, Razorbill, an imprint of Penguin Young Readers Group, a division of Penguin Random House LLC, and Penguin Random House South Africa; The poem 'Gran, can you rap?' by Jack Ousbey, copyright © Jack Ousbey. Reproduced by kind permission; An extract from *I am Malala: The Girl Who Stood Up for Education and Was Shot by the Taliban* by Malala Yousafzai with Christina Lamb, copyright © 2013 by Salarzai Limited. Reproduced by permission of Little, Brown and Company; An extract from *The Giver* by Lois Lowry, copyright © Lois Lowry, 1993. Reprinted by permission of Clarion Books, an imprint of Houghton Miffl in Harcourt Publishing Company. All rights reserved; An extract from *Tuck Everlasting* by Natalie Babbitt, copyright © Natalie Babbitt, 1975. Reproduced by permission of Farrar, Straus, and Giroux, LLC. All rights reserved; Extracts from *Holes* by Louis Sachar, copyright © Louis Sachar, 2008. Reproduced by permission of Bloomsbury Publishing Plc, Farrar, Straus, and Giroux, LLC, and Trident Media Group on behalf of the author. All rights reserved; The poem 'Mosquitoes' by David Campbell. Reproduced by Arrangement with the Licensor, The Estate of David Campbell, c/o Curtis Brown (Aust) Pty Ltd; The Kennings poem, https://www.youngwriters.co.uk/types-kennings, copyright © Young Writers (Part of Bonacia Ltd). Reproduced by permission; A figure from "The Journey of a Rhino Horn", Al Jazeera, 07/10/2013, HYPERLINK "http://www.aljazeera.com" www.aljazeera.com. Reproduced by permission from Al Jazeera; An extract and book cover image from *Refugee Boy* by Benjamin Zephaniah, Bloomsbury Publishing Plc. Reproduced with permission; and The poem 'The Highwayman' by Alfred Noyes. Reproduced by permission of The Society of Authors as the Literary Representative of the Estate of Alfred Noyes.

Photo acknowledgements
The publishers wish to thank the following for permission to reproduce photographs. Every effort has been made to trace copyright holders and to obtain their permission for the use of copyright materials. The publishers will gladly receive any information enabling them to rectify any error or omission at the first opportunity.

(t = top, c = centre, b = bottom, r = right, l = left)

Cover & p1 Tomislav Zlatic
PCM 16 Armation/Shutterstock.com, Formal assessment 1 Bobb Klissourski/Shutterstock.com,
Formal assessment 2 Matthew Cole/Shutterstock.com, Muhammad Desta Laksana/Shutterstock.com,
Formal assessment 3 gabor2100/Shutterstock.com